On the Wings of Prayer

On the Wings of Prayer

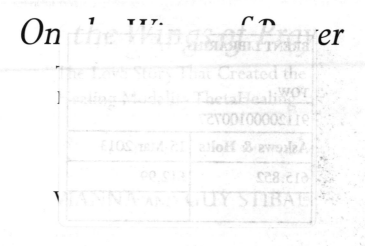

The Love Story That Created the
Healing Modality ThetaHealing®

VIANNA and GUY STIBAL

HAY HOUSE

HAY HOUSE
Australia • Canada • Hong Kong • India
South Africa • United Kingdom • United States

First published and distributed in the United Kingdom by:
Hay House UK Ltd, 292B Kensal Rd, London W10 5BE.
Tel.: (44) 20 8962 1230; Fax: (44) 20 8962 1239. www.hayhouse.co.uk

Published and distributed in the United States of America by:
Hay House, Inc., PO Box 5100, Carlsbad, CA 92018-5100.
Tel.: (1) 760 431 7695 or (800) 654 5126; Fax: (1) 760 431 6948 or (800) 650 5115.
www.hayhouse.com

Published and distributed in Australia by:
Hay House Australia Ltd, 18/36 Ralph St, Alexandria NSW 2015.
Tel.: (61) 2 9669 4299; Fax: (61) 2 9669 4144.
www.hayhouse.com.au

Published and distributed in the Republic of South Africa by:
Hay House SA (Pty), Ltd, PO Box 990, Witkoppen 2068. Tel./Fax: (27) 11 467 8904.
www.hayhouse.co.za

Published and distributed in India by:
Hay House Publishers India, Muskaan Complex, Plot No.3, B-2, Vasant Kunj,
New Delhi – 110 070. Tel.: (91) 11 4176 1620; Fax: (91) 11 4176 1630.
www.hayhouse.co.in

Distributed in Canada by:
Raincoast, 9050 Shaughnessy St, Vancouver, BC V6P 6E5.
Tel.: (1) 604 323 7100; Fax: (1) 604 323 2600

A catalogue record for this book is available from the British Library.

ISBN 978-1-84850-970-2

Printed and bound in Great Britain by TJ International, Padstow, Cornwall

In the Fire of life,
The Fire that lights the darkness,
We are compelled
To ascend,
To rise as sparks,
Rising into the darkness,
Only to fall into Shadow.

Endlessly, we rise and fall,
Bound to karma,
Bound to fate.
We accept that this is life,
This is Destiny.

Yet,
Once in the Fire of life,
There rises a spark that does not dim,
A spark that rises in spite of despair,
In spite of all the vicissitudes of darkness,
Ignoring the shadows that would snuff it out.
It ascends, and does not go out.

As the phoenix from the ashes,
It rises and does not dim,
Beyond all hope,
Despite the very essence of desolation,
The spark pulsates and glows,
Burning with an unquenchable fire,
Rising into the sky,
Becoming the star that lights the way
For others to follow.

The breeze of Creation
Lights the Fire of life.
The embers glow and the Fire kindles.
The sparks alight and rise into the darkness
And do not go out, are not extinguished.
They are drawn, as moths to a flame,
To the star that is resolute,
That speaks to the spirits of the world,
With the voice of divinity on Earth.

Do not despair in the darkness,
Kindle the courage inside.
In fearless intensity, burn brightly.
Ascend, as I have done.
Become a star in the darkness.
Become light,
Until darkness winks out,
And the darkness, quenched, is no more.

Written for Vianna by Guy on the island of Kauai, Hawaii,
at the first ThetaHealing Intuitive Anatomy certification seminar, 2005

CONTENTS

PREFACE

This book is the true-life story of a sacred union of souls. When Vianna and I came together, it seemed as though we were flying on the wings of a prayer and other forces were guiding us, taking us forward in spite of any reservations we might have had. With the devotion and commitment that can only arise from such a union, we were able to create something very special: the healing modality that is now called ThetaHealing®.

The formation of a healing modality has its own very peculiar challenges, some of them considerable and many of them beyond the spectrum of common experience. Vianna and I have encountered joy, heartache and challenges in our personal and professional lives, leading us to create modes of healing for our personal growth on many levels of existence – spiritual, mental, physical, and emotional. This is our story, a humorous, whimsical, melancholy, and honest compilation that is dedicated to all those romantics out there who still have the courage to believe that love can last the ages. May it inspire you never to give up on true love.

Guy Stibal

Chapter One

VIANNA'S STORY

I believe that we all have a destiny. I believe this with all my heart, and I believe that all the events in my life have led me toward my destiny. I have felt this way from the very beginning of my life. To tell that story we have to travel back to before I was born, when my mother was very sick and fighting for her life.

When my mother was pregnant with my sister Elaine, she became very ill and vomited constantly. The doctors thought she had a lack of vitamins and gave her injections, but after the birth of my sister, she continued to be very sick. She went to the hospital and the doctors suggested she have exploratory surgery. During the surgery, it was discovered that her gallbladder had ruptured, which had caused a major infection. The gallbladder had to be removed.

My first memory in this existence is of this surgery. When I accessed the memory through hypnosis, I found myself floating above my mother, looking down on her on the operating table. I could hear the surgeon joking around with one of the nurses, asking her out on a date. Then a tiny fetus was discovered: me. The surgeon said to the nurse, 'You can kiss this baby goodbye.'

Even as a fetus, I experienced a feeling of defiance at this statement. I thought, *Wanna bet? I will live!* But in fact I almost died during the operation. I believe that it was through this close experience with death that I brought my psychic abilities into this life. This experience was also to set the pattern for my association with the medical profession.

When my mother came around from the operation, she was told that she would never carry me. I had a one-in-a-million chance of survival. But my mother, bless her, stubbornly refused to give up on me, and somehow life found a way. I was born on January 12, 1963, in Provo, Utah, determined to survive on this planet.

Just a short while ago my mother said to me, 'Vianna, you are my one-in-a-million baby. Look into my eyes and bond with me. We never bonded when you were born because I had never thought I would carry you.'

I had never felt that there wasn't a bond between us, but this seemed to make her feel better.

My Mother

The influence my mother has had upon my life is unmistakable. She herself has had a very hard life. She was born to an Iowa farmer originally from Kentucky, who lost his farm in the Depression. After working on other farms, he went to work for the railroad and my mother was sent out to work as a housekeeper. She was married at the age of 17.

Mother never drank or smoked, although most of her family did, and at the time it was unusual for someone not to do so unless they were devoutly religious. She taught herself to play the guitar and was a wonderful musician. She made up her own songs and, like most of her family, could play almost anything just from listening to it. Her brother played the guitar and the banjo. I guess this came from their hillbilly roots in Kentucky. At one time my mother would play music for extra money in bars. She has belonged to many different bands during her life.

Her first husband was named Harold. He was the father of my three older half-siblings, Mark, Mike, and Monica.

After she divorced him, my mother met two Mormon missionaries and was so impressed with them that she decided to become a Mormon and move to Utah. In Utah she met Lavar Wilkinson, who was to become my father. They were married, and my sister Elaine and I were born. Due to irreconcilable differences, my parents were divorced when I was three.

My mother then married a man named Richard and had a child also named Richard, who was known as 'Little Richard.' Richard was my stepfather from the time I was five years old until I was eight. He was a good man and treated us decently, but my mother divorced again and married a much younger man named Danny.

At first Danny treated my mother well, but as time went on he became abusive toward her and beat her quite often, to the point of breaking her nose on several occasions. He also whipped my sister and me with belts and often locked me in a vacuum closet as a punishment.

My two older half-brothers had already been sent to live with their father, and during this chaos Monica was sent to live with a different family, leaving Elaine, Richard and me in this rather difficult situation. I was the only one of us who would run for help when a dispute between my mother and Danny erupted into violence. I think the others were more afraid of my mother's wrath than they were of her being beaten; every time you ran for help, you would get into trouble for letting other people know about the abuse.

It took my mother several years to gain the strength to break away from this dysfunctional relationship. For years I had no idea why she stayed as long as she did, but now, as I reflect upon this time in her life, I think that she became caught in a spiral of co-dependency.

Nevertheless, my mother was undaunted by these failed relationships. She always provided for us and stood firm in the face of a society that frowned on divorcées. She often worked at ironing laundry and cleaning houses, and at night she learned how to type. She finally went back to school and became an English tutor and a paralegal. After Danny, she never relied on a man again. I think she was looking for a love that was real, and she was a strong woman who deserved to be with a strong man, but she never found him. I admire her for her courage.

When it came to religion, she was raised a Baptist, and when she converted to the Mormon Church she had the dual belief systems from both religions. That meant that we were raised to believe that if we weren't going to hell for our sins, surely everybody else was.

Mother read the scriptures every day, and when we were younger she read them to us, too, so to this day I have a good grasp of them. She wanted us to listen carefully, and I think she tried very hard to make us good. Now that I am older, I am grateful to her for this. She taught me how to pray and she taught me how to sing. She would play her guitar and we would all sing songs together as a family. She also made sure that we performed in every church event possible. When we were little she would put us girls in fluffy dresses and position us on either side of her in church. If we began to squirm around, she would pinch us to make us keep still.

We spent most of our young lives cleaning and tidying the house. My mother was compulsively clean, to the point of weekly cleaning the closets, pictures and window frames. She didn't believe in mops – she said the only way to truly clean a floor was on your hands and knees. Monica is still the same way – she will even take the light switch covers off to clean behind them and get up in the middle of the night to clean the dust from the dishes in the cupboards.

Mother believed in discipline and didn't spare us the rod. She would use whatever was handy to maintain peace and harmony – yardsticks, broom-handles, even shoes. If you could dodge her for the first few minutes, though, she would calm down. I was the first to figure this out. The other children would stand and take it, but not me – I would run and hide anyplace I could find, generally under the bed so she couldn't reach me. Mother weighed only 115 pounds but could still hit harder than a woman twice her size.

We had a difficult time when I was growing up, and money was tight. When I was 13 we didn't have anything at Christmastime and I remember how this affected my mother. Years later, I went through the same experience myself and decided that I would never let it happen again.

I always felt something was terribly wrong with the situation I found myself in. When I was 13 or 14, while dusting the already clean furniture I would look into the mirror and ask myself, 'Why don't these people know who I am? Why doesn't my family rescue me?' I felt that I belonged to an ancient Egyptian family and somehow they would find me.

I remember thinking that I wanted people to love me, but it seemed that they were too busy or too much in their own world. I realized then that they couldn't love me because they didn't know how, or they didn't love themselves, or they didn't know how to receive love. Even at this early age I knew that I would have to love them so that they could learn to love others. And as I watched my mother and her failing relationships, I knew that I wasn't going to settle for anything other than true love.

My Heavenly Father

As I mentioned, my parents were divorced when I was three, and as a child I rarely saw my father, so I never really had a father figure to speak of, but my mother taught me that I had a heavenly father who was always ready to listen to me. I was also told that he watched everything that was going on in my life. So I established a relationship with my heavenly father when I was very small. As time went on I came to trust this connection to the point where I anticipated results from the information that I heard from my heavenly father.

My mother was always talking about 'Jesus this' and 'Jesus that', but at first I couldn't figure out how he related to my heavenly father. I would think, *Why pray to Jesus when I can talk to the Creator? Isn't that who we should be talking to?* I got myself into trouble with these youthful questions, so I soon learned to keep my mouth shut. As time went on, however, I came to understand why people talked about Christ and other prophets.

At one of the church conferences the speaker brought up the subject of soul mates. He said that there was no such thing and that we shouldn't wait for someone we might have known before in heaven, but instead should settle for someone who was available and make the best of it. Even though I was very young, I instinctively knew that this was wrong and that there was someone out there who was my soul mate. This knowing was to follow me through many years of tribulation and wouldn't go away even when I attempted to reject it and settle for less than true love. I believed that true love did exist, just as in the storybooks. My sister wanted to be a schoolteacher, but all I wanted was to fall in love.

We did a lot of moving around while I was a child. I would go to one school only to be pulled out several months later to go to another, and this wasn't conducive to learning.

My mother had no idea how to deal with teenagers, so when we reached that age we were all sent to live with our respective fathers except Richard and Monica, who were sent to different families.

By that time I was a little wild. I had been traumatized sexually and been too terrified to confide in my mother. This caused me to detach emotionally from her. I became a runaway and when I returned home I convinced my mother that I could move out of the house at the tender age of 15, only to fail miserably. It was during this time that my friends dedicated a song to me, a practice that was common in Colorado then. That song was 'Tiny Dancer' by Elton John.

As a result of my failed attempt at living on my own, I was sent to live with my father in Utah. Elaine had already been living with him for a year, but I had only visited him four times in my life, so I didn't really know him or his wife or what kind of reception I was going to have.

I found my father to be an unusual person. As a young man he had loved to gamble, drink and flirt with the ladies, but he had always understood the value of work, and made Elaine and me get jobs when we moved in with him. One of his rules was that you could smoke cigarettes, but you had to buy them yourself. He did his best to keep the peace at home but always let his wife determine his life and was emotionally abused by her. She was one of the cruellest women I ever met. She took the control knob off the heater and the blankets off the bed, locked up the food in the freezer and only kept bread and butter available on the kitchen counter. She was so mean that even her little poodle would hide its food. I have no idea what she did to make that poodle feel as though it needed to cache food, but I knew how it felt. Every night she had dinner ready at five and if you weren't home, then you didn't eat but you still did the dishes. This didn't work out so well for my sister and me, since we had jobs. As in all the best fairytales, my stepmother made my life very miserable.

Chapter Two

MY FIRST LESSON

I had been living with my father for about six months when I met Harry, a blond-haired, blue-eyed, good-looking man who was to become my first husband. His family was very different from mine: we would go over to their house and they would feed us.

Harry proposed to me two weeks after he met me by writing the words to 'Baby, I'm-a Want You' by the rock group Bread in a letter. His family was concerned about him wanting to marry a 16-year-old girl as he was 21, and my father told us that we had to wait until I was 17, but my mother gave her approval right away, so we dated for seven months and then we were married.

We had nothing to our names. We had no furniture; we used cardboard boxes for tables and slept on mattresses from the dumpster. The first apartment we lived in was a horrible place. About two months later we moved to a one-bedroom apartment. Harry worked as a cook and brought home food from the kitchen. That's what we lived on. His mother and father would give us potatoes.

We had been married for nine months or so and I was pregnant for the first time when Harry noticed that I was having difficulty reading. This was because I had moved around too much as a child to learn properly. Harry stimulated my reading abilities in a crafty way: he brought books home and read them to me, and then, when he had got me interested, he stopped at a particularly good spot and told me, 'Now it's your turn to read the rest.' This stressed me out to no end! But because I was so intrigued by the story, I started to read and comprehend better. The book Harry started with was *The Hobbit* by J.R.R. Tolkien, and the next book he brought home that stirred my interest was *The Lord of the Rings*. This was even more difficult for me, but it was such a good book that I got through it. It was in this way that I started to take an interest in books.

Things had changed in my young mind. I was married and I was going to be a mother. Now I became more involved in religion. My father-in-law gave me an old copy of *Jesus the Christ* by James E. Talmage. The book fascinated me with its insights into aspects of Jesus that I had never known. One night while I was reading it I began to ask the Creator the questions I had about it. I nodded off to sleep with these burning questions in my mind; it was then that I had a dream that was so strong it was a vision.

In the vision, I was taken to a beautiful beach far away. I intuitively knew that the beach symbolized the sands of time and the waters the sea of knowledge. The incoming waves were breaking on a black rock on which a man was sitting. I knew that this was the man himself, Jesus the Christ.

He said, 'Hello, Vianna. We *know* one another.' Then, after a slight pause, he added, 'You have questions about me and my life?'

I said, 'Yes, Lord, I do.'

Jesus waved his hand and said, 'Look!'

In a vision within the vision he showed me all he had experienced in the time before the crucifixion. I saw the Sadducees and the Pharisees, the Romans and the Apostles. He showed me that he understood all of these people and bore none of them any ill will. He was the kindest person I'd ever met. An incredible feeling of compassion emanated from him.

I asked him about the end of the world and when it would come. What I saw wasn't what you would expect: I saw special children being born into the world. This would be the end of the world as we knew it and these children would be the new beginning.

I was so impressed and humbled by the incredible compassion that I felt from Jesus that I decided that I would be as kind and compassionate as he was, or at least strive to be so.

I felt that I must give this incredible spirit a gift for his compassion and mercy and the testament that was his life. I asked him what I could give him.

He told me, 'Vianna, the greatest gift you can give me is to create something beautiful.'

So I made a vow to God and Christ that I would paint two pictures: 'The End of the World' and 'The New Beginning.' Then I had a vision of three murals that I would paint in the future.

This vision gave me a broader perspective of Jesus Christ, and I realized that Jesus and God were not separate parts but belonged together in an incredible totality that was beyond our imagination.

It was after I had this vision that my father-in-law provided the next step in my spiritual evolution: he gave me a tape-recording of a speech Matthew Cowley had given in 1953, at the end of his career. Matthew Cowley was a Mormon missionary during both World Wars. He served as mission president in New Zealand for seven years and in 1945, after his return to Salt Lake City, he was ordained as a member of the Quorum of the Twelve Apostles.

It was during his time in New Zealand that Mr. Cowley showed that he had incredible healing abilities. He would put his hands on people and they would heal instantly. It is said that he actually brought a man back from the dead.

In the tape I was given, he talked about the power of faith and the power of God. He told stories of how God had healed people through their faith. As I listened, I knew that his words were true – faith in God could heal anything. From that moment, I put that faith deep in my heart and carried it with me, particularly when my life became difficult. The tape inspires me to this day. Years later I discovered that according to my father's mother, Mr. Cowley had healed her brother and saved his leg from being amputated.

Harry was a very intelligent man. He could pass any course he took with only a minimal amount of study. This made life difficult for him, however, because he was generally smarter than the people he worked for. He got a job at a firm of operating engineers and we finally bought a $25 couch, but by the time our son Joshua was eight months old, Harry had lost his job.

I was using cloth diapers and I had exactly 17 of them. You had to double them up, use one as a burp rag and the rest as changes, and hope that the baby didn't go to the bathroom before you could wash them in the bathtub at night.

I became very good at making bread each day. One of my fondest memories is letting Joshua play in the flour so that he was covered in it.

It was after Joshua was born, however, that I started to have health problems, the first of which was an infected uterus.

As marriages go, things were also not what I wanted them to be. A year after we were married, Harry and I were sealed in a celestial marriage in the Mormon temple to be married forever. This was important to me and I became very religious afterwards. However, Harry immediately returned to his partying ways. There were times in our marriage when he would go on drinking binges and spend the rent money. Twice I bailed us out by selling everything I owned, even selling my wedding ring to pay for a truck we owed money on. Harry's partying ways also put him in other, more compromising positions, and in retrospect I can see that I never did forgive him.

At the age of 19 I had my second child, my daughter Bobbi Jean. It wasn't an easy pregnancy. I spent most of it waiting on the couch for what seemed an eternity for Harry to come home. He would get off work at 11 PM and show up at 4 AM, drunk.

Around this time I had a very strange experience. We had moved into a new apartment and every day I heard a baby crying in a corner of the room. The noise was very distinct; it was just as if there was a crying baby in the room with me. Thinking the noise was coming from a child downstairs, I asked my downstairs neighbor if she had a little baby. She said no, but the lady who had lived in my apartment before me had lost one.

I thought that the baby had a message for the mother, so my neighbor called her and asked her to come over and talk to me. I found she didn't believe in God or anything spiritual. It seemed that after her baby died, she lost her money, her marriage – everything. She told me the room where I heard the crying was the room she had kept the baby in. The message from the baby seemed to be one of comfort; it was a way of lifting the grief from the mother. The baby wanted the mother to know that it was all right. When I told her this, she began to cry and seemed somehow comforted.

I had used my psychic abilities to help someone. This experience was one of the sparks that got me thinking that giving people readings would be viable.

When I was 20, I had appendicitis. After the surgery, the doctors told me not to get pregnant for a least a year, but my daughter Brandy had different ideas. She was conceived while I was using birth control and condoms. She was born a blue-eyed, blonde-haired baby with a sunny temperament that has continued to this day. But afterwards I had to have a hysterectomy, because my uterus had prolapsed and had almost fallen out. By this time I was 22 years old and my little body had seen its fair share of surgery.

Because my mother had conquered so many adversities in her life, I thought of her as a perfect person. One day, when Harry and I were living in Springville, Utah, my mother and I decided to climb a mountain behind my house with my young children in tow. I remember how proud I was to show Mother how well my family could climb the steep incline, especially as she had fallen behind. When I reached the top, I chose a fast way back down – sliding on my bottom on the sandy portion of an old streambed. As I slid past my mother, I told her that this was the best way down. She yelled that she didn't have to slide like that, but just a few seconds later she passed me, sliding on her bottom down the rocky portion of the slope and cursing as she did so. She cursed only rarely and I yelled at her, asking her what she was doing. She yelled back, 'This is not intentional!' At that moment my mother was no longer flawless to me, but a real woman, a real person.

Harry started to work full time for Fred Meyer department stores and became an assistant manager. From that time, we were constantly on the move with his job. For a time we separated and he went back to his mother, but she sent him back to me to apologize for his behavior. For the sake of the children, I decided to try one more time to make things work.

We never did actually fight, because whenever an altercation arose between us, Harry would simply clam up and not say anything to me at all. This was frustrating, because none of my concerns were ever acknowledged and nothing ever got resolved. Nevertheless, when we moved to Idaho, we did our best to make a fresh start.

The biggest problem that Harry and I had at this point was probably his work ethic. There were several stages in our marriage where he drank alcohol to excess, but mostly he worked so much that we just didn't see each other. When he was home he was good with the children, but it was a rare event that he was home when they were. I have great memories of playing games with my children, but most of these were without Harry. A man does have to work, but there should be time for the family as well.

Even though I honored my marriage to my children's father and I loved him as much as I could, I knew that something was missing – a great love, a love that was deep and passionate beyond human understanding, a love that I had experienced before and would experience again. I also felt that once I met that man again, we would know each other.

It was at this time, when I was around 26 years old, that I began to have dreams and visions of a man who lived in Montana. They were all romantic dreams – not a single one of them was of a sexual nature. In fact I have never had a sexual dream in my life. Nevertheless, I felt guilty about these visions. Harry and I were now able to buy a house of our own for the first time and it looked as though things were going to work out really well for us. So my common sense told me I really didn't want my marriage to end so that I could run off with my dream man.

I started working at Fred Meyer, too, in their herbal department, and learning all I could about herbs. I was relatively happy during this time. Eventually I decided to get a job at Idaho Supreme, a potato manufacturing warehouse. That wasn't so great, as I ended up in Quality Control, doing shift work with women who rivaled my stepmother in meanness.

Then Harry lost his job at Fred Meyer, and all of a sudden he just gave up. When I told him to go and find work, he just told me he wasn't going to. And when I told him that they would take the house from us if he didn't, the only response I got was: 'So what?'

In retrospect, I think he had become chronically depressed and I might have been able to help him had I known more about the disorder. As it was, thinking that the house was lost and Harry had given up forever, I filed for divorce.

I moved into a trailer home with my children. A year later, Harry was tragically paralyzed from the waist down in an accident at work.

Harry had taken me away from a difficult situation with my father and stepmother and moved me closer to my destiny. My time with him was admittedly difficult, but it wasn't all bad. He gave me three beautiful children, and in his own way he was a good teacher for me. After our divorce, we always worked things out between us as they pertained to the children. Recently he allowed me to do healings on his legs and was able to move them in front of one of my classes.

Although stressful, these early experiences prepared me and gave me strength for the rest of my life. I often refer to this stage as 'one of my past lives.'

Chapter Three

NEW BEGINNINGS

Throughout my life I have had a broad range of spiritual encounters, ranging from premonitions, apparitions and strange noises to visions both waking and sleeping, generally with witnesses present. Quite early on I came to the realization that I was always going to have experiences with spiritual energies, and whenever apparitions became annoying, I simply sent them to the Light of God. This always worked very well for me, I think because I have always believed that it is God who is the deciding factor in all things, both spiritual and material, and since I also believe that I am connected to God, apparitions must listen when I tell them to go to God's Light.

This kind of encounter was one of the most consistent psychic experiences I had when I was growing up, but as time went on, the visions about the man from Montana became stronger, both in dreams and waking states. The man had brown hair and blue eyes and was a rancher or a farmer, though I couldn't decide which one it was. When I first dreamed about him, I knew that he was married to a woman with dark skin but that they would divorce. As the time drew near for our first meeting, I knew that he would be driving an old blue and white truck and that he would have a young boy, but for some inexplicable reason I couldn't reach him directly. Time after time I asked the Creator what his name was, but I was told simply that he was my 'guy from Montana.' My intuition told me that he would come into my life when I was ready for him.

As it was, at the Idaho Supreme potato warehouse I met a man named Brett. He was the first person to ever tell me I was beautiful. This was such a wonderful experience for me. It made me feel good about myself for the first time in my life.

With Brett I learned to enjoy the outdoors, to hunt wild game (which fed my children during the winter) and what it meant to have a stable family. Brett was very lucky to have his mother and father behind him. We would go on camping trips to the mountains, riding four-wheelers through forests that I hadn't known existed.

This relationship opened my heart, and when this happens to a person, other people can feel it. As a consequence, other men began to pay attention to me. This made Brett very jealous. As our relationship progressed, he told me that he was having dreams about losing me to a tall man with brown hair and blue eyes.

As for me, I was beginning to have premonitions about teaching large groups of people. I knew that somehow this is what I would end up doing. I could also see that I wouldn't be with Brett then. But I didn't have complete confidence in these visions.

I had moved around too much in my turbulent childhood to have had a decent chance at education, but now I quit my job at the potato warehouse, went on welfare and went back to school. I must admit that I was terrified by the prospect, but I had aspirations to be a volcanologist. Volcanoes had been a fascination of mine since I was a small child. I knew that I was a good psychic and I thought I could use this talent in studying them.

I got my GED (high school equivalent qualification) and in the process found out that I wasn't stupid after all, but very smart. I started thinking of going to college, but the reality was that becoming a volcanologist required at least a four-year degree, and I had little children to care for. I didn't know what to do.

A more immediate problem was that I had to move out of the place I was living in because the owner wanted to sell it.

The RV

I was in a panic because I couldn't find other rental properties. I was terrified that my children would be on the street. I called my father and my sister, but neither could take my children until I could find a place to live. However, my father told me that he had an old RV that I could use until I found somewhere.

In the middle of an Idaho winter, I went down to Utah and drove the RV up to Idaho Falls. The defroster didn't work, so I had to wipe the windows every 15 minutes. Brett's parents let me park in their driveway. My children and I lived there for the next three months while I looked for a house to live in before I started school. I had a voucher for a discount on a house and I had the money to pay the rent through the state, yet no one would rent a place to me. There just weren't any properties to be had, because the navy had moved in for training at the Idaho Nuclear Engineering Laboratory outside town.

I remember living in the RV as traumatic, but to my daughters it was fun. They felt that it drew us closer together. They remember the games we played and the songs we sang. My beautiful daughter Bobbi took over the job of getting everybody up and dressed for school and making breakfast when she was just nine years old. She stepped into a mother's role early in life and has continued it to this day. She has been the rock that has held my little family together.

My son, who was a little older than his sisters, had more of a difficult time living in the RV. What he remembers is that we had nowhere to go.

At one point the heater in the RV broke down, and this was one of the most difficult events of my life. That was when I decided I would never be in this position again.

To help me out, my mother sent me subliminal tapes on many different subjects, ranging from improving memory to raising self-esteem. I began to listen to these tapes all the time and made my children listen to them as well. They helped me to develop my self-esteem, and I can honestly say they made a difference to my life.

I finally found a place to live out on Canyon Road, Idaho Falls, a former trailer home that had been gutted and made into a house. I was able to leave my life of limbo, get my stuff out of storage, and move in.

It was around this time that I heard that the government was required to hire a certain number of women for the Department of Energy...

New Skills

My plan was simple: become a security guard at what was called the SITE at the Idaho Engineering Laboratory out by Arco, Idaho. I knew that the bus ride to work would be long, but the pay and benefits would be worth the effort. They would enable me to support my family and follow my new passion of painting. Then, once I got my Q clearance with the government, I could move anywhere. Even Montana.

I was inspired to begin painting when I was 27 years old. I found I could paint anyone because I could capture the way that the light cascaded across their face and hit their eyes. Over time, painting became my passion. I didn't take classes, just picked up a paintbrush and started off. I would have given a painting instructor fits in any case, because I mixed watercolors with oils and painted with my fingers. I broke every painting rule in the book.

I had always been very protective of Brandy, as she was my last child to be born. She had a lazy eye from the time she was two years old. Over the years we treated it off and on, but as she got older she had a difficult time focusing and her eyesight became worse. She wore thick glasses, and even a patch over one eye at one point, but finally she was referred to an eye specialist, who found that she was going blind.

The specialist, Dr. Box, was one of only a handful of doctors in the United States who could perform a new procedure to save Brandy's eyesight. He was so concerned about her that he told me that he would perform the surgery and would take payments in installments, but I would have to pay the hospital. The hospital, however, was not so compliant over their share.

This was a problem, because I had recently lost my Medicaid because I made $50 over the limit.

I had very little money and no one to help me, so I went to my local church to ask the bishop to do a healing on Brandy. In the Mormon Church, hands-on healings are done through the priesthood.

I asked the bishop, 'Will you heal my child's eyes?'

He told me, 'We don't do healings like that anymore.'

I said, 'Look, you are a member of the priesthood. Put your hands on her head and you can heal her.'

He repeated, 'I'm sorry, but we don't do that anymore.'

I said, 'I have enough faith for both of us. If you just touch her, she will get better.'

He said, 'I'm sorry,' and sent me away.

Devastated, I knew that this was nothing more than a reflection of his lack of faith. This man was a Mormon bishop because of the social aspects, not because of a calling.

I was also confused. I knew that God could heal, but I had been taught that it was the priesthood who did the healing. Yet I felt that God was connected to everyone. I didn't understand how it was only the priesthood who could heal.

I called everyone in my family, including my boyfriend, but no one was able to help me financially. I went home and prayed fervently all night long, troubled as to what to do.

In the early hours of the morning, when I was finally falling asleep, I got my answer. To my dismay, instead of granting an instant healing, my heavenly father told me to go to a state agency to fight for the funds for Brandy's surgery. I was terrified of conflict and humiliated by the thought of pleading, but God told me, 'Lick up your pride and get a hold of your fear. It isn't about you, it's about Brandy.'

Gritting my teeth, I went down to the agency's offices and pleaded my case. To my surprise, they agreed to assist me with the surgery. This was a miracle to me. The surgery was done and my precious Brandy was healed.

This situation served to strengthen my resolve and my faith. I decided that I would never again depend on other people's faith – or lack of it. If I wanted anything done, I would ask God myself.

That was how I started my readings: I would go up, ask God and be told what kinds of things a person needed in their life and needed for their body.

Nuclear Security Training

From 1991 to 1992, I went through the full course of nuclear security training (NST) at the local technical college. Competition was fierce and I had to learn skills that pushed me to the limit. I was at odds with most of the class because I was a 28-year-old woman with children and they were 19-year-old men who wanted to kill something. I knew I was in the wrong course from the very beginning. But if I passed, I would be guaranteed a government job.

During the training, I was required to spar with the men. A few tried to hurt me and I had to toughen up very quickly. This was a difficult time for me.

What I learned from this course was that there were some truly evil people in the world. I learned about terrorists and watched criminal trials and films. This was extremely hard for me.

One of my instructors observed what I was going through and told me, 'Vianna, you don't belong in this course. You remind me of one of those flower children who sits in a field and meditates all day.'

In spite of all this, I stuck it out. I learned hand-to-hand combat, how to shoot a pistol and an M16 rifle, how to use a PR 24 (police club) and how to communicate with people in a stressful situation. I also learned about nuclear safety, defensive driving, non-verbal communication and dealing with a terrorist threat.

Physically, I was required to run a mile and a half in so many minutes. It was very difficult for me to run because I had asthma. But there is a trick to everything in life and running is no different. Brett taught me the proper way to run, and for practice I would run down a long stretch on Canyon Road. Up the road and back again was a full mile. I would run this stretch twice and Joshua would bravely ride his bike with me to protect me. There was a time when I ran with a small pistol in my backpack for safety.

One day I was running with Josh and I twisted my ankle. The pain was intense and made it impossible for me to put any weight on my ankle. Although only 12 years old, Joshua practically carried me all the way back to our trailer home.

Josh himself was very good at sports, but I couldn't allow him to do any school sports because of the extra cost. I have always felt that this was a chance that was denied Joshua, who might have been able to get a sports scholarship to college. I felt he really needed an active father at this time in his life, but this was impossible because Harry was in another state and in a wheelchair. I think that it was because of these feelings that I was to marry my next husband, James.

Security Services

After passing my year-long training course, I took a job working for Security Services of Idaho, a firm which was contracted to businesses around the area. I was sent to work as a security guard at a nearby manufacturing plant until my Q clearance came through from the FBI. This clearance can sometimes take up to two years and be harder to get than a top-secret clearance. The FBI investigates you for things like debt problems, drug abuse, shady friends and associates, gambling problems and the like, all going back over 10 years.

I started out working the midnight shift, then I was moved to daylight hours and eventually I became a sergeant and was responsible for 27 of the other guards. However, I soon decided that doing security shift work at manufacturing plants didn't offer the future that I wanted. I was often away from my children and I felt that in the event that I did get the job at the SITE, it would still be the same shift work I was doing now and my children would be raising themselves.

Part of my job was to greet people as they entered the building. The company liked to have me in this position because I was pleasant to people. After a while I began to sketch the people who worked there and give them short psychic readings while they were on their breaks. I was accurate in these short sessions, and that was when I realized that a business doing this kind of work would be successful.

At this time I had a dream about a Native American man who was herding hundreds of horses down a path in the high mountain canyons. They were coming towards me as I was sitting in a tree, cradled in the branches that overhung the trail. Sitting beside me was another Native American man. As the herd of horses passed by under the tree, the Native American I was sitting beside looked at me, met my eyes, and said, '*Do you know what time it is?*'

The force of this message brought me to the realization that it was *time* – time to leave Brett and move into my life's purpose. Brett had all the right words, but right actions needed to follow, and that was something he couldn't do at the time. I was in love with the idea of being in love, but I knew that this wasn't real love. It was what I would later call a 'carrot' relationship, designed to lead me to my destiny.

Chapter Four

THE CAREER CHANGE

One day as I sat at my desk, absently doodling, suddenly I knew that the next person who came through the door was going make a difference to my life.

That person was called James. He was a security guard, too, but had a longer history in law enforcement and the military. He was the quality-control manager for the company. When he found that I was a spiritual person, he began to pursue a relationship with me.

I liked James, but I wasn't in love with him. I have to admit that it was good to have him around, though, since I had a neighbor with a criminal record a mile long who had begun to be the local Peeping Tom. When I complained to the police, I found out that they had tried to catch him on numerous occasions but had always failed. They attempted to help me this time, but to no avail. When I told James about my situation, he often went and checked on my children for me while I was at work.

James was very kind to my children and also very kind to me. When he began to date me, though, I was dubious. I told him that I was waiting for my man from Montana. He dismissed this, telling me that I had dreamed this person up and he probably wasn't real.

James proposed to me to Roy Orbison's song 'Anything You Want, You Got It.' Thinking practically, I decided to marry him.

I had been manifesting someone to be my friend and watch John Wayne movies with me. That's exactly what I got when I married James. He was good to my kids, and when we were married and he moved in with me at the place on Canyon Road, he dressed up in his camouflage clothing and stalked the stalker. This put a definite end to the situation. Yet with all this, I still held out hope for my dream man.

It was when I was living with James that I decided to open my own business. In a strange sort of way, it was during my relationship with him that my psychic abilities began to increase. Not that he was supportive: he landed a job as a police officer and wanted me to become a dispatcher for the St. Anthony Police Department and eventually a police officer, too. Although I did become a police reservist for a time, I knew it wasn't for me. James once joked with me, 'You want to heal them, and I want to arrest them.'

My decision to change careers from security to alternative healing wasn't based solely on ethical considerations. Health problems were an added incentive. For two years prior to my NST training, my right leg had been swelling up intermittently. When I went to a doctor, the condition was diagnosed as gout – a form of arthritis. This was a strange diagnosis, since women hardly ever got gout and it was rare to have it in the upper part of the leg, but there it was.

This swelling was part of the reason why I took a correspondence course from Clayton School of Natural Healing in 1994. The course included massage, herbalism, iridology, reflexology, acupressure, nutrition, vegetarianism, fruitarianism and the legal ramifications of being a naturopath in different states.

Armed with this new knowledge, I went on a diet without sugar and white flour and then a vegetarian diet. I also used different herbs in an attempt to stop the swelling in my leg and to improve my overall health. The vegetarian diet didn't appeal to me, but my condition improved somewhat and this got me thinking that I could open up a shop in Idaho Falls offering naturopathic consulting and therapeutic massage.

James didn't like this decision of mine and still wanted me to take up police work. The more I became involved in my new idea, the more the two of us began to drift apart.

I came to the realization that I was following my life's path when doors began to open for me. I met a psychic and she decided to give me a free reading. When I gave her a reading in return, she said, 'Honey, you're pretty good at this. You should do this.'

She wanted to leave town to be with her husband, but she was in a lease contract with a massage therapist and had to find someone to take her place. She asked me if I wanted the office.

I was a little uneasy about leaving my job as a security guard, but I saw it as an opportunity, so I told her that I would take over the lease. I am glad that she saw my potential.

When I went back to my security job and told my captain, he thought I was crazy to leave a full-time job to open my own business. I was a sergeant by this time and they needed me.

Nevertheless, I quit the daytime job and gave up my rank to work 12-hour shifts on the weekends so I could schedule appointments during the week. It was hard work, but as if by magic I had an office to work in, and from the very first day I had clients. In fact they were more than clients, they were friends. Within the first week I had met the woman who was to become my best friend and had booked clients for repeat readings.

I started my office with little more than faith, even without much furniture. Because of this, I would have my clients sit on the floor and they thought it was all part of the reading!

It was during these readings that I found that if I listened, the voice of the Creator would give me instructions. So I became quite good at the readings and was asked to do classes on the technique I was using. That was how I started out as a medical intuitive.

From that time onward, my metaphysical experiences increased exponentially and would finally shape the person I would become.

Ancient Memories

All my life I had waited to be certain ages that I felt would be landmarks in my life. These ages were 27, 29, 31, 33, 34, 35, 37, 41, 42, and 47.

It was on my 31st birthday that I remembered a Native American past life. I assumed this was the memory of an ancestor. It concerned a woman who was married with one son. Her husband was one of two brothers who were candidates for the leadership of the tribe. One night the other brother snuck into the husband's tepee and killed him while he was asleep. Though it seemed as though this was so he could be the leader, I got the sense that it was really out of pure hatred.

Once this man was the leader of the tribe, the woman's doom was sealed, because she knew that he had killed her husband. He ordered her and her child to be banished from the tribe.

For a time, the two of them lived off the land. Then a man from another tribe found them in the fields, took them to his village and made the woman his wife – or rather his slave, because he was very cruel to her and beat her all the time.

Then the son of the tribal chief fell sick. The woman had a natural gift for healing, so she went to him and worked on him until he was better. When she returned to her husband, he was furious and started to beat her again. But by this time her son was older. He jumped up and killed the man, stabbing him in the back to save his mother.

This incident caused great turmoil in the tribe. A life for a life was their law. But since the woman had saved the chief's son, he took her and her son to a field, gave them a tepee with provisions and left them there. They were condemned to stay there forever upon pain of death. But members of the tribe would bring meat and drop it off before winter, so they wouldn't starve.

Other tribes in the area thought it strange that the woman never left the field. They assumed she was either crazy or a healer and brought some of their people to her to be healed. Over time, more tribes observed this and starting doing the same. The woman would work on the sick people and sometimes they would get better and sometimes not.

This was her life for many years, until one day a very handsome man was brought to her. She healed him and the two fell in love. They had a child together, a daughter. He asked her to leave with him but she refused, so he stayed with her in the field.

One day members of his tribe came and told him that many warriors were gathering for a battle and he was needed. He went away, leaving the woman with her two children. After the battle, his dead body was brought back to her. This was almost too much for her to bear.

After this tragedy, she sent her daughter to live with her father's people, the Sioux. Her son decided to leave as well, breaking his vow to never leave the field – a vow he had made with the Crow tribe. The Crow were the enemies of the Sioux. The woman stayed because of the promise that she had made to those that had banished her to never leave the field. By this time it had become her place of power and she was one with it. Her only company was an old man who came down from the mountains from time to time. He had gone there to await his death but hadn't died. He taught her many mystical things, including the correct way to make a medicine bag, and many things about herbs. He even gave her a spiritual name: 'She Who Talks to the Wind.'

To the end, the woman never left the field. She stayed there until one day she died all alone.

This was the memory I had. It wasn't a good one or a bad one, simply a memory. But it was so real that I could feel the ice on my fingers in winter. The only person I ever shared it with was my friend Chrissie.

The first thing I tried to do when I started my healing practice was to communicate with the other alternative healers and massage therapists in the area. I had such delusions of grandeur! Like so many healers before and after me, I had the idea of creating a co-operative of alternative healers. I was keen to protect alternative healing in Idaho and monitor any laws being passed by the state legislature that might affect us. My other goal was to found a healing center that would run in harmony for the benefit of all. Over time I found that this was a ridiculous and naïve idea – well, at least the idea that everyone would work together was naïve. No one seemed to want to work together. Nonetheless, I kept looking for therapists who would cooperate to create a healing center of some kind.

In this search I ran across an emotional-release therapist. She would tap on people's bodies to release the emotional energy that was held there. Once this energy was released, it would help the overall health of the individual.

As I was talking to this lady, it occurred to me to tell her about the pain I had been having in my chest. My heart had started hurting all the time and I had tried all manner of things to stop the pain, but nothing had helped.

As I was telling the woman about it, she started tapping on my chest and guiding me into one of the healing rooms. I lay on the massage table, and as she tapped, I began to relive a painful experience I'd had when I was married to my first husband. As she kept on tapping, I released the pain of this memory from my chest. She then asked me if my body and mind had any other feelings to release from this time or from another life. To my surprise, I said, 'Yes.'

I was drawn back in time to ancient Egypt. I found myself tied hand and foot, lying upon a sacrificial altar as a man raised a dagger over his head to cut out my heart.

I curled up in a ball on the massage table to avoid the thrusting dagger. At that moment the bottom of two of the massage table legs shattered and one end of the table fell. To her credit, the emotional-release therapist didn't even blink. She followed me as I slid down the table and continued to release the energy from my chest until the session was finished.

As I lay on the broken table, still entranced by the memory, I looked up at her and told her that I had once been born and grown up in a place called Atlantis. Atlantis had once been a star port for a place called Arcturus. At some time in the misty past I saw that along with 11 women and 18 men, I had walked through a doorway from Atlantis to the pyramids of Egypt. We had used these doorways as portals to and from the stars. Others of my kind had come through them and we had taught the people of Egypt many things. One of them had been the art of *healing*. When Atlantis had fallen, I had been trapped in this world because all the gates had been closed and the way home had been lost. I had left a father on the other side. The people of this world had become frightened of those of us who had been left. The very people I had trained had betrayed me and sacrificed me by cutting out my heart.

When I came out of the trance, the emotional-release therapist said that what had happened had been very strange, particularly the legs breaking on the massage table. One of my daughters, who had been outside the room, told us that she had heard a strange screaming – which was odd, because the therapist and I had been whispering throughout our session.

Soon after the session my nose began to bleed profusely. It continued to bleed intermittently for no apparent reason for another three days.

This incident seemed to be a trigger point, because afterwards things began to get really strange in my life. Up until then, I had accepted the possibility of past-life memories, but I had never believed that I would experience them. I also believed in genetic memories – memories passed down from parents to children that aren't only physical in nature but energetic as well. I believed (and still do) that we carry memories from our ancestors. But now I began to realize that a part of me that I wasn't fully aware of had experienced different times and places.

You must understand that at this time I was somewhat closed minded toward certain things because of what I had been taught as a child. I was about to get an eye-opener.

People had already brought me Egyptian gifts out of the blue, and with these gifts I created an Egyptian room to do my readings in. Now I became so obsessed with my Egyptian memories that I tried to remember all the elements of that life. This was like putting together a jigsaw puzzle when you don't have all the pieces. Over the next two years, I periodically attempted to remember everything I could about that place and time. I began to do hypnosis sessions that focused on that memory. The reason I'm telling you this is because people can get trapped in past-life memories or experiences in other places and times that might not even be theirs. Because of this they live in the past and fail to go forward with their lives.

I never found the answers I was looking for using hypnosis, only more confusion. I decided to let things happen in their own, more natural way. If any memories were going to come back to me, they would simply do so without being forced. This was before I knew about using crystal layouts for past-life regression. With these layouts it is possible to see the beginning and the end of these experiences.

Finally I let my Egyptian memories rest so thoroughly that I barely gave a thought to them. Then one day, later in my life, my mind and spirit were ready for the full memories. They all came rushing back to me and I found the answers that I was looking for, together with the realization that then, as now, I was teaching ThetaHealing.

Eventually I moved my office to a metaphysical store called the Blue Unicorn. After I'd had the dream about the woman who never left the field, I had begun to wear a medicine bag that I'd made for myself. At that time I really knew nothing about Native American belief systems, but somehow I did know the correct way to make a medicine bag.

One day a man walked into the store. He was about 65 years old. He came in, talked to me and left.

The next day he came back in and started to talk to me again. This time he said, 'I know you. I knew you in another lifetime, when you were my wife, and I loved you.'

My first thought was that he was trying to pick me up, because there was a pattern in my life of older men doing that. But the next thing he said almost bowled me over. His soulful eyes welling with tears, he told me, 'You are the woman who never left the field. We had two children together.'

In a flash I saw him as the old man who had come down from the mountains to help me from time to time. He had helped me raise my children, but he hadn't been their father.

Standing in the store, he pointed to my medicine bag and suggested I show him its contents. It turned out that each and every stone was identical to what was in his bag. Every herb was the same. The only difference was that I had an owl feather and he had a hawk feather.

He began to cry and told me again that he had loved me in that faraway time. I stood there and watched as his face turned into that of the old man of my vision.

He gave me a stone and told me it had come from Wounded Knee in the Dakotas. He added that if I ever needed him, he would be there. Then he left and I didn't see him again for a very long time.

This was one of the first confirmations I had of past-life experiences. It indicated that perhaps the memories I had weren't genetic but were due to the transmigration of the soul from one body to another.

It isn't always easy to know what to believe. We may remember our past lives, but we may also be able to tap into lives and memories that are not our own. It is possible to remember so many things and tap into so many memories.

The Law of Truth

I knew that I was on the right track, but James didn't share my vision and continued to view my business with suspicion. My short relationship with him was coming to a close because I wanted to keep my new shop and my new life.

I wanted to be a really good reader, and I knew that the only way was to see the truth. I remember sending out the prayer, 'God, please teach me how to see the truth.' It was a few weeks after this that my answer came.

As I related in *ThetaHealing*, one night I woke to find giant faces floating in my house, asking me to go with them to look at something. There was only one possible response to this: I hid under the bedcovers and prayed really hard until they went away. The paranormal was part of my life, but this was a little bit out of my league.

My friend Chrissie took a different view: she thought that it was wonderful and that I should go with them. Finally I promised her that if they ever came back again I would go and see what they wanted. I was uneasy about this, but I'm a woman of my word.

The next night they were back and I went with them to a place where I saw what looked like rows and rows of hay bales hanging from hooks. Every time I touched one, I could see the deepest, darkest secret of someone I was working with in my shop. Then suddenly I could see the deepest, darkest secret of *every person in my life*.

Finally, when I had seen my husband's deepest, darkest secret, I was released from the vision. I was traumatized. I had watched a man who was taking care of invalid children molest them on a gurney. I had watched people lie. I had watched people do things that were just unbelievable. The next day I decided that I was leaving my husband, packing up my children and my car and driving to Montana. I would find a little town and talk to other people as little as possible.

But I didn't have enough money to set myself up in Montana. I had to go to work the next day to earn it. Feelings of doubt were creeping in, but that day God sent me seven people who had been in my vision and each of them confirmed the awful truth.

By the time I had finished with my clients, I didn't have time to drive the four hours to Utah, pick up my kids, then turn around to drive the six hours to Montana. So I went home and went to bed.

The huge faces came again and this time they took me up through what I came to know as the planes of existence and showed me everything that I had done in my life. At that moment in my life I was with a person I wasn't in love with, in a place I didn't want to live in and faced with having to leave my shop because I couldn't meet my financial commitments. I could see all of this and the realization came to me: I had created it.

I had asked God to show me truth and I had met truth. I had met the Law of Truth – it had come into my living-room in the form of faces and balls of formless energy. It had shown me how to see truth. But it had also shown me that I could manifest change in my life. Prompted by the Law, I went through a checklist of the things that I needed to change. I needed a new place to work from and a new apartment – and a new husband. James had been a hero and a friend to me, but we weren't compatible, and now I knew his deepest, darkest secret, I had to leave him. I thought to myself, *I want my man from Montana, the man I always dream about.* But then I stopped myself, saying, 'Oh, but I'm not ready for him yet. I don't deserve him yet.' See how my beliefs limited me!

Within two weeks I had moved into a brand-new apartment, moved my shop and gotten a divorce. As for the man who was to become my next husband, I had already met him. Be careful what you wish for – you just might get it!

Chapter Five

BLAKE... AND CANCER

Blake was a client who came to me for a reading in 1994. Although an odd-looking man (short, balding, and with a cleft palate), he had striking blue eyes and a bizarre sense of humor. He had married his childhood sweetheart, Paula, and he and his brother had gone into business manufacturing candy machines and made a lot of money. One of their employees, Maggie, had been his fantasy woman. He had carried on an affair with her for two years, but eventually she had wanted more from the relationship, so he had divorced his wife and married her. Soon they had problems, however, and Maggie left.

Now Blake was visiting psychics in an attempt to procure some kind of magic potion to bring her back to him. When he came to me, he asked if she was ever going to come back to him. I told him straight: 'No, Maggie will never come back to you.'

Little did either of us know that I knew Maggie from nuclear security training. She had claimed then that she was being stalked by her ex-husband. Now the ex-husband himself was telling me that he had hounded her for over a year and a half. Looking back, I can see that he was entrapped by love for more than one person.

When you do readings for people, it is much easier than usual to see where they are coming from. You can feel their pain and you see them without judgment. You have a compassion and understanding for them that you wouldn't have in everyday life. I felt this compassion for Blake, and I could see that he needed help to free himself from the situation he had created. I did my best to guide him toward a path that would liberate him.

Apparently I was the only psychic Blake had been to who had given him solid information and not just what he wanted to hear. He suggested that we help one another in a business sense and offered to trade me renovations on my office, including installing an air-conditioner, for continued psychic readings.

Little alarm bells went off in my head, but since it was so hot in my office without an air-conditioner, I agreed to the renovations. Then, when I moved to a new office space, Blake added an infra-red sauna and helped to make my room presentable.

He was interested in metaphysics and told me that he and his brother dabbled in hypnotism. Since I was hungry for knowledge, I permitted them to hypnotize me in order to discover things about myself. Blake had been taught hypnosis by his brother and had no other formal training at that time, but he seemed to be good at it.

While under hypnosis, I could see many things, but some of the statements I came up with were rather bizarre. In one session, one of the brothers asked, 'What is my life's mission?' and I answered with a series of numbers. They didn't understand this until they consulted engineers who told them that I was giving them the coordinates to travel to distant constellations.

In retrospect, I can see that these hypnosis sessions were a perilous undertaking. I allowed Blake just a little too far into my subconscious mind and I think he took advantage of it, and of my naïveté. However, he had a lot to offer in the way of knowledge about the subconscious mind, and as we came to know each other, he seemed to be a kind person.

He asked me what I was looking for in life and I told him that I wanted to find absolute truth. He said he would help me find my answers if I would help him find his. That was when the energy started between us.

I told Blake that I believed in the Mormon religion. He had been raised a Mormon as well, so it surprised me when he asked me, 'What do you believe in that you would be willing to die for? Would you die for your religion? Do you really believe everything they tell you?'

I couldn't answer. This kind of thinking was beyond my experience. I had thought that Mormonism was the ultimate truth, but recently I had been having experiences that had begun to expand my consciousness.

Blake helped me to realize that there was a whole world of belief systems to explore, and they weren't necessarily 'evil' or wrong simply because they weren't sanctioned by the Mormon Church. Had I heard this from a person who wasn't Mormon, I would have dismissed it out of hand. But this kind of thinking brought me to the understanding that I could love all religions and find truth in them all.

One day Blake's first ex-wife, Paula, came in to talk to me. She had been following Blake around like a lost puppy since their breakup, in spite of the fact that she had married a man in the military. He had now been stationed in another state and she had to leave with him. She asked me to take care of Blake while she was gone.

I didn't know quite what to make of this, but it made more sense afterwards when Blake became preoccupied with me. I told him that we shouldn't date, but he replied, 'Why date? Why not get married?'

I said, 'I am waiting for a man from Montana. I have been dreaming about him. He is going to be in my life and I am going to be with him.'

Blake said that the person that I was dreaming about probably wasn't real and that even if he was, he didn't care. Until I found him we could be together, whether it was for a week, a month or a year.

Initially I was suspicious, but I believed that Blake had good intentions towards me and sincerely felt that we would be good together. He also knew that in order to be with someone, I had to have marriage in the picture or I wouldn't consider having anything to do with the person. So marriage seemed like a logical decision. Even my mother approved, and she hadn't approved of anyone I had been out with before. This should have been an indication to me *not* to marry Blake!

Some of you may wonder why I didn't see what was coming in my life. That is a skill that I only developed later.

So, on that note, Blake and I were married in November 1994. The first week was good and the second was fine. A month later the weirdness began. On Christmas Day, who should show up but Blake's ex-wife Paula, at six o'clock in the morning, to watch us open presents.

It wasn't difficult to realize that Paula was still attached to Blake and there were things going on behind the scenes. I was concerned, but nevertheless Blake convinced me to take Paula and their son along with us on a Christmas vacation to see his parents. Looking back, I have no idea how he did this. Maybe I hadn't learned how to say no and didn't know what it felt like.

On the trip, I could tell that Paula still loved Blake. When we had a moment alone, I told her that she needed to move on. However, within a few months she had left her husband, moved only five blocks away and was coming to our house every day.

I knew I was in the wrong situation, but I didn't know how to get out of it. Paula was always there, even on weekends, and I came to suspect that Blake was encouraging her to come around. It was very unsettling, particularly when other people began to warn me about my husband.

It was certainly true that Blake was one of the strangest people I had ever met. He would create drumming rhythms on almost any surface. He would sleep only 15 minutes a night. He thought he knew a great deal about hypnosis and in the first year of our marriage he hypnotized me almost every day, telling me it was to make me the best psychic I could be, although I found out later that it was more about getting the winning lottery numbers from me. There were also dozens of times, later on, when I would be all set to leave him and he would talk me into a quick hypnosis session and suddenly I would have feelings for him again.

The positive side of the relationship was that I learned a great deal about poverty consciousness, and Blake convinced me that I could have the things in life I wanted, no matter what I had been raised to believe. As an example of this, he took me grocery shopping and told me that I was worthy of having the best food rather than the cheaper alternatives. He taught me that if I thought I deserved something, I would make enough money to buy it.

Nevertheless, our relationship was a strange one, to say the least... In retrospect, I think that Blake could feel my dissatisfaction with the marriage and this made him increasingly difficult, which in turn made me increasingly dissatisfied. The friction inside me kept growing, and less than a year into the marriage I was admitting to myself that I had made a mistake.

That wasn't all. Over the years I had heard people say that their relationship was killing them, but it wasn't until this marriage that I understood what they meant...

Cancer

My leg had continued to swell up periodically, and it was getting to the point where I couldn't walk on it. This as much as anything hindered me from ending my relationship with Blake. In August 1995, I found myself once again sitting in a doctor's office.

Dr. Davis was an older doctor and had a lot of practical experience. He examined the leg, drained out the fluid that had built up in it, then took an X-ray. Afterwards he told me that it looked like a tumor and referred me to a bone doctor named Edward Biddulph.

Dr. Biddulph was very kind to me, but he had bad news: 'I am very sorry. You have a malignant tumor.'

Blake and I sat in silence for a moment and then I asked the doctor, 'You mean cancer?'

He said, 'Yes, I mean cancer.'

Blake asked, 'Is it terminal?'

'Yes, it's terminal.'

Blake said, 'What's the next step?'

Dr. Biddulph told him, 'There is no next step if it's in her lungs. I have only seen two cases like this one, but sometimes amputation can help.' He turned to me and said, 'The amputation could give you a little more time to live if it hasn't moved to your lungs.'

As you can imagine, I was appalled. I didn't know if I should believe the doctor or not. I didn't know exactly what was wrong with my leg, but it didn't feel to me that his diagnosis was entirely correct. However, the test results were undeniable material proof, at least to him.

That day Blake and I went to the local hospital for a chest X-ray. When we arrived, my heart was beating fast and my nerves were on edge. I told the X-ray technician she shouldn't take an X-ray right now because I was a psychic and I knew from past experience that I had a tendency to break machinery when I was upset.

She laughed and told me, 'Honey, this machine cost the hospital millions of dollars. There's no way that you can mess it up.'

She stopped laughing when she began to take my X-rays and the machine just quit.

After finally taking the X-rays with a much older machine (when I had calmed down), she took my business card and later became one of my favorite clients.

That same day, Dr. Biddulph found that there were no problems in my lungs and suggested I schedule an appointment at the University of Utah for further tests.

When I got home, my next-door neighbor came over to visit and began to tell me about the problems she was having with her boyfriend. When I told her that I had just been diagnosed with cancer and was terminally ill, she said nonchalantly, 'Vianna, I'm really sorry about that, but can you give me any advice about my boyfriend?'

In that instant I knew that it really didn't matter to anyone else that I was sick. As I continued talking to my neighbor, I started to absently doodle on a piece of paper, as I sometimes do. When I realized I had doodled the word 'heal' upside down, I became determined to find a way to heal my body.

Later that same night, a terrible thunderstorm sent the temperature plummeting. I remember sitting down by the heating vent in the hall to coax some kind of warmth into my body. I was despondent beyond words and I began to pray. I felt that I had too much to accomplish on this Earth to give up so easily. In confusion and sadness I sent forth a cry to the Creator: 'Why me? Why am I losing my leg? God, am I going to die? I have so much left to do!'

In reply, I heard a voice, as loud and clear as if someone was standing right next to me in the room, saying, 'Vianna, you are here with or without a leg, so deal with it.'

I didn't know it at the time, but this was just the answer I needed.

On August 22, 1995, I left Paula to watch my children while Blake drove me the four hours from Idaho to Utah for a bone biopsy. During the drive, I felt as though darkness was gathering about me.

At the hospital the nurses had heard that I was psychic, and I automatically began to do readings for them, giving them advice. Then they sent me to an internist so he could gather a case history. He asked me all kinds of questions about my medical history and said he disagreed with the initial diagnosis of bone cancer, saying the results were inconclusive. Next I was sent to the surgery room to be prepared for the biopsy.

Because I had asthma, the doctors used a local anesthetic and I was forced to listen to the sounds of the hammer and drill as the surgeons took a sample of my femur from the inside, as you would when you take the core from an apple.

During the procedure, one of the nurses, in an unprofessional slip, asked the doctor, 'What *is* that?'

He replied, 'I've no idea. I've never seen anything like it.'

What they had found was that about six inches of the inside of my femur appeared to have dead bone cells in it.

As I was leaving the hospital, the doctors warned me that if I put too much pressure on my leg it could easily break. If this happened, there would be no alternative but to amputate. I was to use crutches for the next six weeks. I was also informed that I might have only a few months to live.

When we arrived home the next day, I found Paula preparing dinner for my children, dressed exactly like me. Terribly sick, I listened to Blake and Paula whispering in the next room about how she was going to take my place at my business.

Enough was enough! I was going to care for myself.

First let me say that I have never been against conventional medicine. I believe that we should respect the opinions of trained health-care professionals, and in most cases they are likely to be correct. Even so, I felt that in my case the doctors were wrong in their diagnosis of bone cancer. I thought it was something else, but I didn't know what.

The information I was receiving from the Creator was that I should clean my body out, so I started putting my knowledge of naturopathy to good use and doing cleanses. To his credit, Blake agreed with me on this. I began with a lemon cleanse, which I did for 18 days although I threw up for the first three. It seems I had developed an infection in my leg, probably from the biopsy.

Although I was on crutches, I still gave readings, and no one seemed to care, since I still did a good job. I did massage on one leg, pushing my other leg onto the table as I moved around. I even taught classes during this time, sitting on a chair in front of the class because I couldn't stand. During the last week I was on crutches, I did a psychic fair. But I was in unbearable pain and my life seemed to be falling apart. I hobbled around, wondering how much longer I was going to live.

I remember waiting for the test results to come back with a great deal of anxiety. I was lying on the bed when the phone call came, with Blake and his ex-wife in the room. The University of Utah explained that the tests were inconclusive for bone cancer because the biopsy had only shown dead bone. They had to send the results to the Mayo Clinic for more comprehensive testing. They told me that they were certain that I had cancer, but they didn't know what kind, and they wanted to schedule me for another bone scan. I agreed to go down for one more battery of tests.

As I digested the news from the hospital, a bittersweet resolve rose up inside me. Looking at Blake and his gloating ex-wife, I said to myself, 'I'm not going to die, I'm going to live, and you two are going to be stuck together forever. I'm going to get better, divorce you and move on.' I gritted my teeth and mapped out a recovery plan.

I'm sure that Blake must have been wondering what to do with me. To his credit, he began to use essential oils and hypnosis on me in an effort to help me heal.

Back at the University of Utah for the bone scan, I was sitting in a wheelchair waiting to be seen when I overheard a gaggle of doctors discussing the X-ray and MRI results of a patient. It seemed she was in really bad shape. *Poor woman,* I thought. I found out later on that they were discussing me.

I had a very bad reaction to the radioactive iodine that they gave me for the scan and almost stopped breathing. I threw up, and the doctor ran in to check on me. When I had stabilized, I told the orderly that I had to go to the bathroom. He took me to a toilet on what he called the 'chemo floor,' where they administered chemotherapy to cancer patients. When he wheeled me down the hall, the feeling of death was all around me. That was when I made the decision that I wasn't going to have chemotherapy.

At the end of a very long day, I went home to await the biopsy results from the Mayo Clinic. I continued with my alternative therapies, researched remedies for cancer and used essential oils, hypnosis, subliminal tapes, different foods, and Essiac tea. It seems that when people find out you have cancer, they send you all kinds of literature in the mail, and I received offers for 100 different therapies.

A couple of weeks later, the University of Utah called to give me the results from the Mayo Clinic. They had determined that I had some kind of lymphatic cancer or undiagnosable bone cancer and that was what had killed the cells in my femur. When I heard this, I knew it to be the truth. I also knew that mercury poisoning had caused it. Why? Because I went up and asked God, and was told I had been poisoned by mercury.

The doctors suggested that I schedule chemotherapy and/ or radiation treatment as well as another biopsy. I told them *no*. Apparently they scheduled me anyway and later called me to find out why I wasn't there for my treatment. Again I told them I wasn't going to have it.

This decision was at least in part based upon the fact that I already had a huge bill from the biopsy, I had no insurance and my husband had refused to pay for further treatment. If I had chosen to undertake the chemotherapy, the only way to have gotten it would have been to divorce my husband, sell my shop and go on Medicaid – and then, if I had lived, how would I have cared for my children?

I felt more alone than I ever had in my life. To be fair, this must have been a terrible trial for Blake, too. He must have been confused and horrified. I'm sure he had never anticipated having to deal with a new wife who was dreaming of someone else and refusing to allow a replacement in her office, even though she was terminally ill, his childhood sweetheart wanting him back and hoping his wife died, the prospect of new medical bills which could mean he lost everything, and, on top of all this, Maggie coming to him for a loan. He had to borrow that from Paula.

When I stopped using the crutches, I walked with a limp because my right leg had atrophied and was now about three inches shorter than my left. Each step I took was painful. Still I continued to see clients, not because of great courage or endurance, but because I had financial obligations and my young children needed me.

Throughout this time, my children were never far from my mind. I felt that I had no one to send them to in the event of my death. My marriage to Blake was anything but a true partnership, and I knew I couldn't rely on him. Besides, my children stayed in their rooms most of the time and wouldn't interact with Blake. Where could they go? The very thought of them being brought up by relatives, even their (paraplegic and ill) father, was unbearable. These thoughts gave me the will to live. I couldn't just give up and die, leaving my children alone. I had also grown very attached to my shop. That, too, was my baby, my creation, and I just couldn't let it go.

But in spite of everything I was doing to help myself, I remained very sick. Sometimes I really thought I was going to die. Then I would tell myself, 'I can't die, I haven't met my man from Montana yet.'

The constant pain made it difficult to rest or sleep, and when I finally did get some rest, it wasn't complete. I often dreamed of running with a pack of wolves in the mountains, seeking my man from Montana. Somehow I felt my soul mate was in the same area as the wolves, and I wanted him to know that I was doing my best to make contact with him again, and if I died before I could find him, I was sorry. I would dream of him constantly, seeing him on a tractor and driving an old pickup.

As time went on I came to envision myself running with the wolves because when I did the pain wasn't so severe. I would imagine floating out into the wilderness, drawn again and again to the wolf pack high in the mountains. At first I saw myself as a human running naked with the wolves, but when I was going through one of the sauna cleanses, I was so exhausted that I finally went into a deep hypnotic sleep and found myself going inside the alpha female as I ran with the pack, literally merging with her. I didn't feel the pain at all when I was in her nurturing body and could get some kind of rest. So this became a routine for me.

As the wolf pack ranged the area where I felt the man from Montana was, I began to use their energy as a bridge to his dreams. I would run to him in his dreams, but there was some kind of barrier between us. I couldn't get into his dreams, but I could sense the dreams of his little boy. So I would run into *his* dreams and try to get him to tell his dad that I was coming. But I would speak to him in the form of the she-wolf and the boy would be frightened. This would make me feel bad and I would leave.

One night as I was running with the wolf pack, the female wolf that I was running with got shot in the hip by a rancher. The pain was intense, but she limped off and got away. The alpha male, however, a black wolf I had come to know, was shot and killed. Two days later, I read in the newspaper that two wolves had been shot close to Yellowstone Park, where they had been among a rancher's cattle. A black male had been killed and the lead female had been shot in the hip. I thought this was very strange. But what was truly strange was that I couldn't walk for several days because of a pain in my hip.

The pain from the cancer was still agonizing, and when people from my local area heard of my plight, they came from seemingly everywhere to help me. One man came into my office and offered to heal me. He put his hands over my leg, began to shake all over and made strange noises, contorting his face as he did so. When he had finished, he told me with intense conviction: 'Now you are healed!' I thanked him, but I wasn't any better.

At this time in my life I was dubious about most energy healers. I felt that unless the healing was fairly immediate, I shouldn't waste time with it. However, there were two people who came to help me, Alice and Barbara, who were wonderful and gifted energy healers. When they gave me Reiki sessions, I was out of pain for several hours. Their skills kept me going through those dark times and I still thank God for their help. They would come up for several days in a row just to help me, and I'm sure their prayers kept me alive.

I was a pitiful sight at this time, hobbling into my office, leaning on my massage table and painfully struggling through readings. My marriage continued to be painful, too, since Paula was always there. I could only assume she was waiting for me to expire. It must have been terrible for both Blake and Paula, wondering what was going to happen to them.

As my leg had shrunk so much, the doctors told me that if I did survive, I would need physical therapy in order to walk correctly again. Yet despite this, I believed to the core of my being that God could heal me in an instant. In fact, I felt that I already knew how to heal myself. There was just something I was missing. I had used conventional medicine, cleanses, nutrition, oils, vitamins, affirmations and visualizations... what was it?

Every time I asked the Creator, I was told that I already knew the answer and that I just had to remember how to call upon God. But I *couldn't* remember. Throughout that long, hard winter of 1995 to 1996, I continued with alternative therapies and went to work to pay my bills. Blake had brought the infra-red sauna home for me to use and I spent a lot of time in it. We put it in the garage, and one time Blake accidentally locked me in there for six long, stressful hours. I will never forget the pain I went through before my children came home and let me out. They say that you forget pain, but they are wrong – you never forget bone pain.

Throughout these dark months, I was clearing the poisons out of my body, but I had no way of clearing the emotional poison of Blake and Paula's relationship. I told Blake to get her out of my home, but he ignored me. Regardless of what was to happen to me, I resolved that somehow I was going to leave Blake.

As I related in *ThetaHealing*, the answer to my prayers came while I was in the mountains in May 1996. At that point I was in trouble. The pain had gotten worse and my leg had begun to swell again. I knew that if I didn't find the answer soon, I would be dead.

At that time I used to stage potluck dinners once or twice a month for several reasons. For one thing, the local metaphysical community didn't get along very well, and sharing food seemed to ease the competition and personality clashes. These gatherings also helped to stimulate my business and the businesses of the other healers in the area. I wanted to have one last potluck dinner, so I organized a gathering up above Heise Canyon.

My aunt Jackie showed up unexpectedly from Oregon, but became very sick with a stomachache. She lay down in a tent she had pitched and I hobbled inside to help her, thinking to myself, *Oh my gosh, she's going to ruin my last potluck dinner!* I went out of the top of my head through my crown chakra, as I would do when giving a reading, and when I was in her space I asked God why she was sick. The Creator showed me that it was giardia, an intestinal parasite. I told it to go away and witnessed the Creator releasing it. Within seconds it had gone. This gave me food for thought.

The next day a man came into my practice with a severe backache and I repeated the procedure on him. Instantly, his back pain was gone. That night I decided it was time to do the same thing to myself.

The following day, as I hobbled to my office, I stopped about six feet before the door, went out of my space through my crown chakra and prayed to the Creator. I then commanded a healing on myself, and it worked! My leg returned instantly to its normal size and the pain disappeared.

The first person I called was Chrissie, and then I called Blake, who told me not to get my hopes up. He was convinced that the problem would come back, no matter what had happened. I must admit, I was apprehensive about the pain coming back, but it didn't. The Creator had healed me.

I believe that everything happens for a reason. So I asked myself what I had learned from my experience with cancer. I came to the realization that I had spent my whole life taking care of others, never buying or doing anything for myself and always doing what was expected of me. Now I knew that I had to take care of myself *first* and then I could take care of others. I decided that I was going to live my life to the fullest, and I wasn't going to waste my time with things that didn't bring me joy. I began to plan how to get out of my marriage.

Blake had plans, too. When he saw that my leg was healed, he perceived it as a goldmine. I told him that I thought the technique could be taught to other people, but he wanted to keep it to himself. He said that I should go on the lecture circuit and do healings but not teach anyone the technique. But I wasn't going on any lecture circuit because I knew that this healing technique was supposed to be for everyone, rich or poor, especially the common men and women of the world. I told Blake, 'When God says it is time and people invite me to teach them, I will go out and do it.'

The ThetaHealing Technique

I started using the technique on people with all sorts of diseases and infirmities. Many were healed instantly, others took a few sessions, and still others simply did not heal.

I knew the results could be improved if we had a better understanding of what we were doing, so I commenced investigating. That's when I came to believe that the healings were being performed from a Theta state of mind. I had some knowledge about this state because of Blake. He had many books about the subconscious mind and was obsessed with the Theta brainwave.

Using the Theta state for healing wasn't new. Many hypnotists had brought clients and health practitioners to that state in order to perform healing. I was taking it further, though: I was convinced that you could call upon and connect with God in that state, and that would lead to amazing results. If my theory was correct, then I had a breakthrough in healing and an explanation of faith healing that could be scientifically measured.

I began to teach the technique in the classes that I held locally. During my first class, a student stood up and told me that it was absolutely impossible to hold a conscious Theta state, as the other brainwaves would interfere. He said that it was a great theory, but was impossible. I was amused by this response and more determined than ever to prove my theory.

As I explain in *ThetaHealing*, validation came in December 1996 when a physicist friend made us an electroencephalograph and I was able to test people. Sure enough, every single person was going into a Theta state while practicing the technique. And not only was the practitioner going into Theta, but so was the person they were working on. It was then that the term 'ThetaHealing' was born.

My daughter Brandy was one of my early test subjects for ThetaHealing. At 12 years old she didn't have one of her front teeth because for some reason it hadn't come through yet. The dentist assumed that she didn't have the tooth, so I commanded that a tooth be created.

I then took her to another dentist for a second opinion. He told me there was a tooth but it was in the wrong place, behind the eyetooth. It seemed an easy fix, so I commanded that her tooth move over and come through. Within two weeks, there it was, and perfectly straight, too. In fact, it was the only straight tooth in her mouth. I attempted to psychically straighten Brandy's teeth, but this was painful for her, so I decided to take her to get braces. When I did so, the dentist told me that he couldn't put braces on her until he had pulled the extra tooth that was growing behind her front tooth. Then I remembered I had commanded a tooth to be created and had commanded a different one to move over – and had never canceled the first command. So the new tooth had to be surgically removed – which Brandy wasn't really happy about!

Brandy always healed fast, though; she had perfect faith. On one occasion when she was in high school, she pulled her arm out of its socket when she was cheerleading. I was teaching a small class at my office when she came in, tears streaming down her face and her arm just hanging there. She walked up to me in front of the class and said, 'Fix it, Momma!'

No pressure there! I remember being horrified, thinking, *I have to take her to the hospital!* But there she was, right in front of my class, asking for a healing. So I excused myself, took her into my healing room and did a healing on her shoulder. It went right back into place and Brandy skipped out of the healing room, walked back through the class and went back to cheerleading practice.

Even though this was a very exciting time for me as far as healing was concerned, I was still very unhappy in my personal life. Sometime late in 1996 a friend of mine sent me to an NLP practitioner to help me gather the courage to ask Blake for a divorce because she, like the rest of my friends, couldn't stand watching the situation.

Up until this time I had been afraid that Blake would hound me the way he had Maggie when she left him, but after my session with the NLP practitioner, I went home and told him I wanted a divorce.

Blake gave me an emphatic *no*. He told me that if I followed through with the divorce, he would destroy my business and my children and me. Although this was undoubtedly just an empty threat made in fear and anger, I backed down immediately.

During this time, I had conversations with God. My truth about the situation and the Creator's were always different. The Creator's truth was: 'These people came into your life and you allowed them to walk all over you. You could have said no or dealt with the situation in many other ways, but in reality, Vianna, you allowed this to happen. It was such good drama.'

To stand in my truth and admit to myself that I was responsible was more than I could handle at the time. I just couldn't do it and continued to come up with other reasons for the situation.

The Creator's response was, 'Haven't you finished yet? Do you want to change? Would you like to know how? You need to release yourself from any obligations you have to this person. Change your belief systems and this person will fade away from your life.'

The Gift from Bobbi

Still, I was hesitant to definitively end the relationship. I was afraid of what might happen, but I also pitied Blake and felt responsible for him in a strange spiritual way. I knew that I had to figure out a good way out of the relationship.

By this time Blake had had a power-coating business but had sold it and had retreated to a room in the house to meditate all day long. His goal was to reach a pure Theta state so that he could manifest anything he wanted. While I felt that meditation was fine, I also understood that in order to manifest something you had to meet the universe halfway and take the action that was needed to make it happen. Blake, on the other hand, wouldn't attempt to do anything – he would just meditate in an upstairs bedroom. Even worse, he would spend all afternoon attempting to put himself into a pure Theta state, and then I would show him how easy it was for me to do it in seconds. Quite understandably, he was furious with me.

Then came the last straw. It was my daughter Bobbi who forced the issue.

Bobbi was always a real trooper, with strong mothering instincts. She had been asking me for a while if she could go and take care of her paralyzed father. I went up and asked God, and I heard, 'No, Vianna, if she goes to live with her father, she'll get pregnant when she's 14. But don't worry, because she'll graduate when she's 17 and all will be well.'

This alarmed me. Bobbi was a good girl and I had never had any trouble with her, but I decided I would watch her closely and not let her go anywhere where she might get into trouble.

In January 1997, on Blake's birthday, Bobbi kept pestering me to let her stay the night at a girlfriend's house. Her friend's parents were going to be there, Bobbi hadn't been out of the house in a while and my friend Chrissie suggested I let her go. There seemed no reason not to. I should have asked God about the situation, but instead I let Bobbi go out.

At 10:30 that night I received a call from the parents of Bobbi's girlfriend, who had just gotten home, and I went over to get her. I could see that she was drunk. I could also tell that she had been taken advantage of and thought she might be pregnant.

When we got home, Blake was angry that Bobbi had gotten drunk on his birthday and began to say cruel things to her. This was the last straw. I had a difficult time standing up for myself, but when it came to my children, it was different. Blake and I got into a heated argument. Suddenly the psychological grip he had over me was broken, and I was able to stand up to him.

When I got Bobbi alone, I pushed her to tell me what had happened. Apparently she'd had nonconsensual sex and she was afraid that she might be pregnant. We went down and got her a pregnancy test and it came out negative. But about four weeks later we tested her again and she was pregnant.

It's really difficult when your child is pregnant out of wedlock, particularly in ultra-conservative southeastern Idaho. The consciousness of the area towards this kind of thing is one of puritanical judgment. I knew that Bobbi would have a difficult time in school and just about everywhere else, so I gave her options. She broke down and cried and told me the only thing she had ever really wanted was to be a momma. She wanted to have this baby – it was *her* baby and she wanted to keep it.

I told her that if she wanted to keep the baby she had to provide for it, and she did. She started working in my little office as a receptionist, and during this time she was home schooled.

There was no point expecting support from the father of the child. We found out later that he had taken advantage of several young girls. In fact, he ended up serving time for statutory rape on several counts.

It was very interesting to observe people's reactions when Bobbi got pregnant. I had friends and students coming to me and saying, 'You can hide Bobbi until she has the baby and no one will know.'

I thought, *You silly people – this is my daughter. I love my daughter. I'm not afraid or ashamed of anything that has happened to her. She is part of our family, and I want this baby.*

As soon as I said this out loud, it changed how people viewed the situation. All of a sudden the psychics in the area were talking about a 'special spirit' that was coming to Bobbi. They were right about how special the baby was. As soon as she was conceived, I had the energy and the wherewithal to get out of a bad marriage.

When Blake found out that Bobbi was pregnant, we got into a big fight over it. When things had calmed down between us, I encouraged him to go to a two-week class on rapid-induction hypnosis so that he could make a living from it. He went, but when he came home he found the house full of my friends. He was furious and sent them all home. Then he started screaming at me and told me that he wanted a divorce. I told him that was fine with me. That floored him.

Later that night he came back to me and apologized and tried to take everything back. But now I had the psychological platform I needed. The next day I filed for divorce.

When I spoke to my lawyer, he asked me what I wanted out of the divorce and I told him that all I wanted was my business, the infra-red sauna, an amethyst geode and a coffee table made of burl-wood myrtle. I didn't want the cars, the rest of the furniture or any money from Blake. I would even take on board all the bills from the University of Utah. The lawyer told me this was the most ridiculous thing he had ever heard. But I told him that I just wanted to get out of the relationship and feel safe.

A week later I served Blake with the papers. At first he laughed and threw them straight back at me. It took a very long time to convince him that I was serious. When I did, he actually chased me upstairs and sat on me for eight hours in an attempt to browbeat me into staying with him. Then he refused to leave the house.

When I had first met Blake I had promised him that I would never forcibly remove him from my house because that is what Maggie had done to him, so it was a difficult situation. Finally he left and moved in with Paula. For a while he followed me around, just as he had done with Maggie. But he has been with Paula ever since. They truly belong together.

With Blake, I was in an unstable relationship with an unstable person. Yet in spite of all the problems that I had with him, I learned a great deal from him. I learned that I had talent, that I was accurate in my readings, and that I could be successful. I learned to change the way that I thought about abundance. Finally, once I recovered from my bout with sickness, I learned that I could be free of Blake and still be successful.

I think that Blake was in my life for a reason. He was there to help me learn that I could overcome life's challenges without having someone tell me what I could not do and then proving them wrong. That had been my way of moving forward in the past. Now I learned there was an easier way.

In the past I had expected the people that I was in relationships with to simply know what I wanted and needed, and my relationship with Blake taught me that I had to communicate my wants and needs... and to be able to say no.

Blake also helped me to define exactly what God was to me. This opened me to the belief that God loves all people and religions equally. For all his positive attributes, though, Blake wasn't a believer, and a believer was what I needed.

Almost 12 years later, when I was in a store with Bobbi, I ran into Blake and Paula by chance. I didn't actually recognize them at first, I think because I had worked on my resentment issues.

I scanned Blake's body and asked him, 'How's your blood pressure?'

He said, 'It's almost under control.'

I looked over at Paula and asked her, 'How's your insulin resistance?'

She said, 'I just barely found out that I had it.'

Bobbi was jumping up and down behind me all this time, and finally she got my attention. She mouthed 'Blake' at me and it was only then that I realized that I was talking to my ex-husband.

At that moment I realized that I had no more resentment or anger, and I'll tell you why: it's because we create our own reality. It's true that these people had hurt me, but I had let it happen because I didn't know how to say no. When I got free of them, I finally took responsibility for my own life.

In all of my relationships before I met Guy, I didn't know how to let myself be loved. I was smart enough to leave relationships that weren't working out, but I also had a definite program that I had to leave them before I found my man from Montana. Maybe I chose people I knew I could walk away from. But now it was time to meet my soul mate again.

Chapter Six

GUY'S STORY

I was born in Dillon, Montana, on April 1, 1960. I was raised as close to the Earth as you can get in these modern times in America, on a working family ranch. From the time I was very young, I had the opportunity to play in the broad irrigated fields of Idaho and the mountains of Montana. These places became my playpen as soon as I had been permitted to escape from the first one.

In those days, our little family of my father, mother and older sister, Sheryl, lived in a mobile home in the Centennial Valley, Montana, in the summer; and on the Stibal homestead in Roberts, Idaho, in the winter. As a small boy of not more than four or five, I would hear the call of the wild beckoning to me like a siren song. It was the owls that did it, the great-horned owls that lived in the huge poplar trees that were all that remained of those my great-grandfather had planted on the old homestead nearly a century before. The owls would call to one another and keep me up at night. Their song awakened me to the fierce Earth mother outside my window, beseeching me to come outside. I would peer out of the window, watching the silver light of the moon dance and create gray shadows, with the overwhelming feeling that somehow I had to get outside. This feeling persisted when we moved into the large homestead house, where I learned to walk on the old wooden floors and to run semi-naked in the fields, free as an animal unleashed from its cage.

As time went on, this need to be outside at night was most prevalent when the moon was full. I can't remember ever being afraid, just alive and free. There were times when I would run so far that I would get tired and curl up underneath a ditch bank to sleep, shivering at the cold of the night like a forlorn puppy.

My parents, God bless them, would come looking for me, calling out in the early morning light, praying I had not drowned in the Butte-Market-Lake-Canal. They would find me, wrap up my shivering little body and put me back to bed, hoping I hadn't caught a chill.

Eventually I learned to escape and return without my parents knowing. It was then that I realized that the Earth and sky gave off a sound of their own. If you stood motionless and sent yourself down into the Earth, you could sense the song of life that it emanated. And if you went out to the stars, you could hear their song as well.

As a small boy, I was given the book *Where the Wild Things Are*, and I think that this helped me to understand that the demons inside people are much worse than anything nature could possibly produce. Besides, I wasn't raised to fear nature, but to have a healthy respect for it.

One of my fondest memories is when I was about six years old and my family went on a camping trip up Peterson Basin on the Gravelly Range in the Centennial Valley. It was mid-August. Once we had pitched camp, a sheepherder came to call. He wanted the beer we had to offer, and I assume that he was a little goofy from being alone for months at a time, since he was boisterous and rather loud. My grandfather talked to him at length and he left for his camp.

The next day, here comes the sheepherder, storming through our camp on a horse, brandishing a rifle and shooting at some imaginary target, shouting, 'There's a bear! I wounded him, but I'll get him!' Off he gallops into the deep brush, once again shooting his rifle.

This terrified the women in camp, since a wounded bear is a definite cause for concern. The men saw it as a practical joke on the part of the sheepherder and laughed it off, but my mother made my father keep a rifle close at hand that night in the tent, I think more to protect us more from the crazy sheepherder than from an imaginary bear.

The next morning, a storm moved into the area, and even though it was August, since we were at an elevation of 7–8,000 feet, it began to snow. Six to eight inches fell very quickly and it was time to head for the lower elevations! The road became a muddy quagmire, the pickup trucks periodically got stuck and we all had to get out and push, even us little kids. That whole day turned into a mild nightmare of stuck vehicles and cold weather, and we were all covered in mud by the time we got down to the valley floor. It was these kinds of experiences that colored my early years.

In spite of all the time I have spent working in the asphalt jungles these last years, I am still a child of the Earth. To this day, I feel the call of the wild places of the world, and I believe that the essence of this feeling comes from the land that I was raised in.

Let's stop for a minute.

'Wild' to me does not imply being unintelligent or uncultivated. To me it describes the freedom we are able to enjoy in this life, hopefully without damaging the freedom of others. My childhood was wild, and idyllic compared to most. It was blue jeans, flannel shirts, pocket knives and .22 rifles. It was real cowboys and Indians who worked the ranches. It was pheasants in the fields, badgers, foxes and gophers in the canal banks, hawks and eagles in the sky, deer, elk, and moose in the mountains, buffalo escaping from Yellowstone National Park. It was fearless cow-dogs and cow-ponies that would not die, no matter how old they got. (One, named Sinner, lived to be 39 years old.) It was fish in the streams that would bend your fishing pole in a half crescent, deer in the alfalfa fields and old arrowheads in the deep sagebrush. It was cattle, and wild horses with manes so long that they dragged on the ground. It was forts made out of straw bales, and my sister's goulash when my mother was working at the local store. It was pilfering my mother's butcher knives to use as swords in my imaginary world, and finding and opening the Christmas presents early and sloppily wrapping them back up. It was the Border Mountains of Montana, and places in Idaho that were wilder still, with primeval forests and backcountry that went on forever. Some of these places made a boy feel as if he was the only person on Earth.

My mother, Sandra, didn't raise me a savage. We went to church every Sunday and to Bible study on Tuesdays, and I was required to have table manners that my mother enforced with an iron fist. Mother and Dad are intelligent, common-sense people who could have excelled in any endeavor they put their minds to. But they were born into long lines of agriculturalists and followed suit.

My God, the endless thundering herds of cattle that I saw at that time! I remember the harsh winter winds, the snowdrifts as tall as houses and watching my parents make trail drives straight through the inclement December weather.

My grandfather Charles was the person who started the whole ranching thing with our family. He disliked farming, largely because his father wouldn't let him ride on the horse-drawn equipment because he felt it was too severe on the horses and made him walk behind. Farming in those days was brutally hard work, and my grandfather opted for a life as a rancher. His love of animals and the high country led him to the Centennial Valley.

One thing that I found interesting about my grandfather was that when something was wrong with the herdsman watching the sheep in Montana, he would know about it in Idaho. When he drove into the mountains, sure enough, he would find that the herdsman had gotten drunk and left the herd untended. This psychic radar proved accurate and consistent enough to be commented on by my grandfather's three children and older brother. Communication was difficult in that day and age, so this kind of talent would have been a valuable commodity.

My grandfather died in December 1969 and soon afterwards I had a dream. In the dream I was riding the school bus home, and the driver, Mel Wildie, stopped just in view of the Stibal farm to open the bus door and welcome in a man who had been standing by the road. I was sitting in the front seat of the bus and Mel turned to me and said, 'Hey, you know who this is, don't you?'

The man got on the bus and it was my grandfather Charles. As he sat down beside me, I got a creepy feeling of fear and revulsion that froze me to the core of my little body. The bus door closed and Mel began to drive away. I felt that there was a wrongness about the whole thing, that neither my grandfather nor I should be participating in the dream.

He asked me, 'Do you know who I am?'

I looked at my feet and nodded my head.

He said, 'There is something that I need you to do for me. Your mother and father will need you. I need you to take care of them for me. Will you do this for me?'

Once again all that I could muster was a brief nod. But I somehow knew that I had taken an oath that was to bind me to the ranch for a large portion of my life.

I woke with the hairs on the back of my neck raised, with the chill that can only come when you have touched the feeling of death.

After the death of my grandfather, my father (also called Charles) and my uncle formed a partnership. After that, we were constantly on the road, managing two properties some 90 miles apart.

Our ranch, like many others, was based on a herd migration. In the winter months the herds occupied the lower elevations in Idaho and in the summer they went via truck to the mountains in Montana. My grandfather had wisely changed from sheep to cattle some years before. We always breathed the proverbial sigh of relief when the herds were in the hills in the Centennial Valley.

My family truly loved the Centennial Valley. It lies north and east of the continental divide along the Montana–Idaho border and rises to 6,000 feet in Beaverhead and Madison counties. The Centennial Mountains are on the south side of the valley and the Gravelly Mountains on the north. The muddy Red Rock river flows through the valley floor, feeding the Upper and Lower Red Rock lakes. The two properties my father and uncle owned there were named after past owners. The Price place was the lower place and the Christenson place was located higher and deeper in the valley, closer to Yellowstone National Park.

To this day, the valley has one of the most intact ecological systems in Montana, in part due to the ranchers who have left it that way for more than a century. Elk, deer, and moose are common, along with many species of raptor. But the very best thing about the valley is the ringing silence. This kind of silence frightens some people from the cities who are not used to it, but there are those who fall in love with it, enraptured by the soundless sound that is quiet yet loud.

This high mountain valley is the very essence of tranquility, and this word best typifies why most people live and work there. Ranchers rarely admit to this, however. Love of nature is a subject they keep to themselves, lest every environmentalist and well-meaning tree-hugger in the nation descends upon their fragile solitude and shatters it.

The rancher lifestyle is based upon two aspects that are so intertwined as to be the same thing: the livestock they own and the land that sustains these animals. I have watched family ranchers and farmers live a lifestyle that is vanishing, much as the Native American way of life did in the late 1800s. The only difference is that in the present day the land encroachment comes not from invaders but from the ranchers' own people in a sort of inverted land grab under the guise of preservation. What many of these well-meaning environmental groups have failed to realize is that the only reason these lands do not have subdivisions and factories on them is because of the rugged individuals who have kept this from happening – the ranch families who have worked the land for generations.

The reason why these ranchers live this kind of lifestyle can be quantified in a word that any Native American would understand: freedom. Freedom and solitude are part and parcel of this vanishing way of life. It was the solitude that I loved best – the quiet of the Centennial Valley where all you could hear was the beating of your own heart and the rustle of the wind over the plain... and there was no other human being for miles.

It is difficult to describe the feeling of quiescence that nature brings to one who has been immersed in it from an early age. You never escape it and you would not wish to if you could. You cannot readily describe it to others; it has a mystical quality that is indescribable, a vibration that is beyond words or thought. You never question this connection with nature once you have it, for it is an understanding that becomes numinous in content – a feeling that begins when you are very small and never leaves you, suffusing all your senses with such incredible beauty that it is almost more than you can bear and beyond the ability of the normal physical senses to experience or explain. When this mystical feeling touches you, you rarely speak of it. It is melancholy, joy, elation, and sadness all wrapped into one. It is many feelings, for nature has many faces. This is apparent to those who can slow down long enough to watch her. Even over a few hours it is starkly apparent how changeable she is. Nature is indeed female, yet there is a quieter male essence that is the hidden part – that element that whispers to us in the ancient symbolism of the green man, the ancient Celtic male representation of nature.

It is possible to temporarily lose track of these vibrations of nature in the vortex of modern technology, until you understand that all technology owes its very existence to nature. Everything that we utilize to create a city comes from nature. When you realize this, you begin to see that humans are more like ants than anything else. Those of you who have observed an ant colony will remember that for five feet around the colony there is nothing – every stick is gone and the earth is laid bare. The ants take all the materials available until they are all used up and the ants have to make another home. But the Earth will prevail, as it always does. The ant pile will return to dust and something else will replace it. I predict that one day the Earth will reclaim the cities and we will return to nature, all in a natural cycle.

The first 12 years of my life were good, but it's only now that I realize how good they were. Then came the time when I began to work. My father was my hero and I wanted to be like him, so when he suggested in his rough way that I start working, I went with him and began to learn how. I can still remember his words: 'Help a guy out, if you can.'

My first initiation into ranch and farm work was cattle branding at the Jones ranch, which was close to ours in Montana. My father and I started in the early morning and, together with other pairs of calf-wrestlers, branded 1,000 of the struggling calves. By the time we had finished, it was near dark and I was so sore I could barely stand. I was covered in bruises, calf feces and urine, but the cowboys treated me like a man. That made it all worth it.

On a ranch everybody works, so the women would be running the branding irons and vaccinating the calves while at the same time organizing the food preparation. Women probably work as hard or harder than men at brandings. Brandings acted as community events for all ages in the Centennial Valley when I was growing up. People would come from all over to share in the excitement of the event, and the parties that came after sometimes lasted into the next day.

The brandings themselves were wild, dirty, and dangerous endeavors and I'm surprised that more people didn't get hurt, particularly when the calves were roped and dragged to the calf-wrestlers. Invariably some fool cowboy would rope a calf by the head instead of the feet, and the rope and 300 pounds of struggling calf would act as a combined pendulum and engine of destruction to knock down people, tables, and branding pots. When this happened, things became more entertaining and dangerous than any rodeo.

Working with cattle is always dangerous, and horses aren't much better – worse in some ways, in my opinion. A good horse is hard to find and you'd better treasure it, because the rest of them are designed by the good Lord to either become chain lightning as you are riding them or act like a turtle in a race with a rabbit.

You may as well know that as a rule, cattle are an accident waiting to happen. They always get themselves into some kind of insanity, ranging from getting sick and/or entangled in barbed wire to escaping to another rancher's herd, turning renegade, and running wild. The term 'domesticated' is a loose one, applied only to cattle that are contained in a strong corral. The longer you leave cattle alone in a large field or in the mountains, the wilder they get. We would get to experience the excitement of the chase as my father and uncle would dash after an animal on horseback and herd it back to the correct pasture, sometimes with the animal destroying several fences in the process.

There was always something to do on the ranch. We were constantly sorting cattle, moving them to other pastures, doctoring, fencing, shipping, calving, haying, and irrigating, regardless of the weather or the season.

Most of it was brutally hard work, the kind that most people could not or would not do. I remember my father once hired two men to help him with the hay harvest. They were big men and gave my mother the willies when they came in for lunch. My father was outworking both of them as they stacked bales of hay and they began to whine about the pace of the work and the magnitude of the harvest that was before them.

As they were loading the hay bales on an elevator for my father, who was on the top of the stack, one of them, waxing belligerent, looked up and said, 'Man, *nobody* works this hard!'

My father looked calmly down from the top of the haystack and said, 'Then I've got no use for you.'

The men left that day.

Our hay bales were put up mostly by hand in those days. The best I could do at first was to roll these bales together into lines to be picked up by my father and uncle. My sister worked at this as I did, and as for my mother, she had bigger biceps than I did until I was 18, and she could outwork me as well.

My mother had always been athletic. Her family came from the Bitterroot Valley in Montana, and her great-grandparents on both sides had come across the prairie as pioneers in the 1860s and '70s. I was fortunate to know my own great-grandparents on my mother's side of the family, and I found the Bitterroot Valley to be one of the best places on Earth, and my mother's family to be some of the best people I had ever known.

Whenever I wasn't working, I would disappear into the hills and fields to explore, hunt, and fish. From when I was very young I had been hunting for Indian arrowheads when in Montana, as had others in my family. I was fascinated by the people who had made them and how they had lived. In time I had a small collection of artifacts and I was interested in all things Native American, to the point of becoming an amateur archeologist when I was older. I even took up flint knapping and hunting with bows that I made.

By the time I was 14, I had begun to practice throwing knives and axes. I learned more about the bow and arrow (re-curve bow) and how to shoot and use all manner of weapons. I was a bit wild and dangerous with firearms until I learned (the hard way) how to use them safely.

At 16, I began to become interested in religion, metaphysics, the paranormal, and, particularly, martial arts. I took karate from a man named Ernie, who taught a form of it from Okinawa.

High school was difficult for me for various reasons, some my own responsibility, some not. One factor was that I was somewhat withdrawn around people. In fact I could be comfortable not speaking to another person for weeks, if not months. This strange detachment from social interaction has followed me through my life – in fact, it is only because of my love for Vianna that I am now social at all.

By 18, I was fascinated with the working of wood, iron, and steel, and I took welding at an Idaho technical college. The new interaction with people in town left me a little confused, however. I see now that I wanted the solitude and purity that only the mountains could bring.

I went back home and worked at a few jobs. Then my father had a heart attack and I went to work at the ranch full time.

It was my feelings of concern for my father that kept me on the ranch, at least at first. As time went on, as well as working on the ranch, I became interested in metallurgy and started making knives and, later, swords.

Before I met Vianna, I was married to a Spanish–Navajo woman named Laura. We were married in 1985 and I adopted her son, Andy, a year later, when he was four years old. A few years later we had a son named Tyrel.

This marriage was difficult for all parties concerned. From the start, there was friction between Andy and me. When he was a child, Andy was defiant as a rule, even when he didn't need to be. I have to admit, he was beyond my ability to handle. My mother spent a lot of time with him and did her best to help him through school. We all did our utmost to help him, but in spite of all my pleas, he thrived on conflict and I couldn't reach him. This situation lasted for many years.

Both boys were extremely challenging children. Both reminded me of wild horses that just wanted to run free.

In 1990, I bought a house and a couple of acres of land in Roberts, Idaho, not far from my parents' place. The house, known as the Eichinger place, was old by western American standards. The core of it had been moved there in 1904 from another location, so it was difficult to say how old it really was. Over time, I came to find that it was haunted. Ghosts would come to the front door to ring the doorbell. You would go to the door and there would be nobody there. There was always someone walking outside the windows on the front porch, too, and there would be myriad strange noises throughout the night. I lived at this place for over 15 years. Now that I've moved away from it, my memories of it are half obscured, seen through the mists of Avalon, a veil of fog and Earth magic.

There was a time when the Earth powers were very close to me, much closer than they are now. In my present line of work, I am somewhat removed from them. Nowadays, I am either in front of a computer working in the square box of an office with long rectangular buildings all around me or I am flying to a distant destination. All of this is removed from the circles of the seasons and the endless progression within nature that I was so connected to when I worked on the ranch. The Eichinger place resonated with these essences, due to the old trees outside. The house was surrounded by box elder, poplar, and black willow, some of which were settler trees planted to establish homestead rights. There were other trees there, too, ones that weren't common in the cold, windswept, high mountain desert of southeast Idaho. Black walnut trees and several other less common varieties made a precarious living in the cold climate, surviving, I think, only because of the shelter of the other trees.

I also loved the peonies, columbines, hollyhocks, and lilac that were planted in different places on the property. There was an apple orchard, also plum trees and berry bushes of all kinds. I loved this little oasis in the middle of farm ground. There was even a little garage that I converted into a shop for blacksmithing and knife-making. The place was perfect to me, at least at the time.

Years later, I found out that the water there had heavy metals in it, especially manganese. When I had my hair tested, I found the levels in my body higher than acceptable. Manganese can cause people to have mood swings, and I assume that this was a factor in the behavior of both boys. Once Vianna and I became aware of this, we started to pull the heavy metals from my sons, and over time they have improved a great deal.

The marriage to Laura lasted for 13 years, and the main reason it lasted as long as it did was because I had been taught that you made a marriage work. Laura was wiser than I was: she wanted to break up on several occasions. She knew that we weren't compatible, but my stubborn 'never give up' attitude and Laura's mother, Mary, held our marriage together.

Both Laura and I did try very hard in the relationship, but we were different people and wanted different things. Laura was unhappy with sobriety, the solitude of the ranch, the long hours, the money (or lack of it), the sweat lodge I became involved with, the martial arts I devoted time to, the total lack of vacations – I swear, you just can't please some people!

In all fairness, I think that Laura also had a difficult time because of what happened to her younger sister, Bertha.

Some people shine with a rare radiance, and Bertha was one of those people. She wasn't just pretty, she was downright beautiful. Laura had helped her mother to raise her and they were bonded in a way that I envied.

She had a mischievous streak, though, and she developed a taste for the bad boys. She married a young man named Shawn, and as time went on it became evident that he was unstable. I went hunting with him on several occasions and found him strange, to say the least. He just wanted to impress me with the man-stalking that he had supposedly learned in the army, and he confided to me on several occasions that he had killed people. He gave me the creeps and when I got a chance, I told Bertha to leave him.

Bertha didn't listen right away. The two of them moved to another town, close to Shawn's mother, but they did break up in the end because of Shawn's violence and jealousy. Laura told Bertha to come to us and that we would protect her, but she refused, as she was staying at Shawn's mother's house. Shawn himself had been incarcerated in a behavioral health center and I got a phone call from him babbling about how he was going to kill Bertha. I did my best to reason with him and he eventually calmed down. It is one of my deep regrets that I didn't keep better track of his whereabouts and wait for him when they let him out. As it was, unbeknownst to all of us, he was released from the center with medication, somehow got hold of a .22 caliber pistol, broke into his mother's house and hid in a closet, waiting for his mother and Bertha to come home. When Bertha came into the room with a friend of the family, he jumped out and shot her and the other lady execution style, in the head, then turned the gun on himself. The family friend was killed instantly, but Bertha and Shawn both lingered for a few days in the hospital.

As you can imagine, the family was devastated. I have never heard such dreadful keening as I heard from Laura during that time. I think Bertha's death destroyed the magic that was once in Laura. She never acted the same way afterwards, and I think she began to look for ways to kill the pain.

The night Bertha died I was outside looking at the stars with tears flowing down my face. Then, as clearly as if she was only a few feet from me, I heard Bertha's voice. She said my name just once, in a plaintive and almost accusatory tone, and then she was gone. Full of regret, I resolved to do all I could to protect those I loved.

The Sweat Lodge

After this, the ranch became an island for me, a hermitage, a refuge from people and from the madness of city life. I would watch the outside world with a jaundiced eye and stay away from it. I would only go to town out of necessity. I would lose myself in ranch life, and Laura and I shut down emotionally toward one another and drifted farther and farther apart.

When I was younger, I had become involved with a mixed-blood Native American man named Joe Cohea who was running sweat-lodge ceremonies. He had been pouring water in his ceremonies for 25 years when I first met him, and it was as if I had come to a spiritual home. Joe had a lot of practical knowledge about primitive arts, and I learned a lot about surviving off the land from him.

I learned from Joe that the sweat-lodge ceremony is pantheistic in nature – traditional natives understand God as the sum of the universe and a mystery to be accepted and not usurped. To them, the Creator pervades all things, flowing like an invisible spiritual liquid that is the essence of life. The differences between mainstream religion and native culture are apparent in that to the native mindset, all life is equal. From the smallest ant to the most massive grizzly bear, all life is important and equal in the mystery of creation that is the hoop of life.

I was involved off and on with sweats for some years before Joe taught me how to drum and sing. Eventually we formed a powwow drum group called Ancient Thunder. Then Joe decided that I should run a sweat lodge myself, much to the discontent, and blessings, of the full-blood natives in the area on both sides of the issue.

Laura and my immediate family were opposed to it. Since Laura had been raised a Catholic, I'm sure that she felt that it was strange. When Joe began to train me as a water pourer, there were some speculations about my sanity. Certainly, my family didn't understand why I was doing it. My parents even sent a spy in the form of my aunt to see just *what* I was doing and whether we were smoking peyote or involved in similar nefarious dealings. (I have never used peyote, nor is it part of any purely traditional sweat-lodge ceremony.)

The truth of the matter was that I had been studying religion, both comparative and mainstream, for some time. In fact, I had been exploring how I felt about spiritual matters from the time I first went to school, when I had watched what happened to children who were of a minority religious orientation. I remember one boy, Brad Morgan, who was a Jehovah's Witness. We became friends, but the other boys in our class didn't like him because he didn't salute the flag or celebrate Christmas. He was a small blond-haired boy and was an easy target for a much larger fanatical boy. This boy beat him so severely that I was afraid for his life, and with each blow the larger boy struck, he cursed the smaller boy's religion.

So, since I had seen discrimination firsthand and recognized it to be evil, I had no wish to judge the beliefs of others. However, I had found them fascinating as a study, and my love of the Earth had made it natural for me to be curious about traditional Native American religion.

Now the sweat lodge was the catalyst for a new life. It was there that I was opened up to healing. Some people misunderstand the lodge. As I understand it, the sweat is based on surrendering to the Mystery (sometimes referred to as the Creator) and being empowered through it. Properly done, the sweat is a place of growth, an opportunity to go through a rebirth, a renewal of the soul and a cleansing of the body and mind. The forces that are unleashed in the ceremony are not toys, but powerful energies that will open avenues for great change. These changes are dependent upon many variables, as they pertain to the universe and its workings, but if you invoke these energies, you can rest assured that something is going to happen.

It is interesting to note that the process is by its very nature a form of belief work. There is the interaction with other people and listening to what comes from their heart. This opens you to introspection and helps you to see your own inconsistencies as well as to release those emotional aspects that aren't for your highest and best. Granted, the sweat lodge takes a lot longer than belief work in a therapeutic sense, but it nonetheless creates change within a person that expands into the world to create manifestations. When you open yourself to the Creator, expect change. If you don't have the courage, don't step up to the challenge.

The realization of this began in 1993–94, the year I was given a way to pour water by Joe. He grilled me for a full year on the do's and don'ts of the sweat that he had 'put up' for me. It is very important for people who put up a sweat to do so in the correct way, as recent events in America have proven. People need to study the sweat for several years with a veteran leader before they pour water. Without this experience there can be dire consequences. I was taught that you never charge money for a 'staged' sweat lodge, and I never have. The sweat isn't a marketplace.

Dreaming of Change

Over the following months I knew on an instinctual level that I was getting ready for something, but I didn't know what it was. I could feel it coming, the same way that I could feel a storm brewing on a clear windless day. It was an itch that I couldn't scratch, causing the hairs to rise on the back of my neck.

I had been courting the thought of leaving the ranch for a while, but I didn't know what I would do instead. What I didn't realize until later was that my future was sending me messages through my son Tyrel. When he was a little boy, Tyrel used to have the most terrible dreams. He would be in different levels of consciousness when he had these 'night terrors' and could be looking right at you and still be in the middle of the nightmare. One thing was consistent: every time he would be screaming about the 'wolf people' who were coming after him and talking to him. One of these wolf people was a female wolf who would come chasing after Tyrel with the rest of the pack behind her.

By 1997 I had been working for my parents' partnership with my uncle for 17 years, and it had reached a point where all I was doing was work. I'm sure that there are others out there raised on family farms and ranches who know exactly what I'm talking about. As the only son, my situation was complicated: I wasn't a working partner but a full-time employee. My father had attempted to make me a working partner, but his brother didn't want anything to do with it, and I felt that there was no future there for me.

Leaning on my shovel, minding my own business, I would let my consciousness float out in a bubble within a dream, off into romance, adventure, and the wild world outside the confines of my self-created solitude. Much of the work that I did was hard, some of it pure drudgery, and this was how I escaped – through the power of my imagination, taking a magic carpet ride in my mind. This was how I kept going – by freeing myself into a living dream, my thoughts floating on the country breeze to be caught by the unseen currents of manifestation. It was this dreaming that was the cause of it all. The only thing more important than dreaming is true love – but isn't that what we dream of?

Vianna and I have a running joke that I am still leaning on that shovel, and my life now is all a dream conjured from the spell that was woven then... and one day I will come to my senses and I will still be on the ranch. There are times when I wonder if all the years since I met Vianna *have* been real, since they have such a surreal feel to them, a feeling that Vianna shares with me. I still wonder if someday I will find myself leaning on my shovel in the year 1997.

~~~

The ranching lifestyle is hard for people who weren't raised in it to understand. There were times when I was unable to get a day off from October to June, and this wasn't conducive to married life. My wife at the time certainly didn't like it, and I'm sure I wasn't making enough money in her estimation either. In 1997 she started drinking again and we separated.

I knew in my heart that it was over. If you have ever given a woman an ultimatum to choose between you and something else, you will know that the something else generally wins. I learned this small wisdom.

When I was going through the divorce, I was an emotional drama queen, but the minute I signed the papers, I was over it! The emotional unsteadiness was gone and I was rebuilding my life.

In my secret heart I was looking for a spiritual woman, a woman I could connect with, someone who truly loved me and was devoted to me. I promised myself that I wouldn't settle for anything less than this high priestess. If I didn't find her, my intention was to become a reclusive monk, or as close as I could get to it and still make a living. Would I ever find her? That was the query I put out to the universe.

It was during this time that I began to go to sweats three or four times a week in preparation for some inexplicable event. I knew that I was being led toward a destiny that I had been waiting for my whole life, so I began to cleanse and purify myself, just as the warriors of old had done before they left home for war.

My years of contemplation in the sweat lodge had taught me many things, and I was starting to manifest change in my life through the personal development of my beliefs. I knew that I had to change, and anyone who opens themselves to God to create change will find themselves in service to God at the same time, on a fused path of manifestation. It can be a perilous thing to open up to God. There is real power out there in the universe.

A few weeks before my divorce, my thoughts were filled with starting a new life so that I could enjoy nature, raise my son, and find the high priestess. I was looking for my soul mate and instinctively I knew that she was finally close to me. I didn't have long to wait, nor did I seem to have much choice in the matter, as I was swept into Vianna's life with a synchronicity that was too powerful to ignore, much less reject.

Chapter Seven

THE MAN FROM MONTANA

Vianna

When I divorced Blake, my life changed. My daughter and my son's wife were both pregnant and living in my house, and I was working full time (and overtime) to support all of us.

Bobbi always encouraged me, saying, 'Everything will be all right, Momma.' Somehow Shawn Mullins' song 'Lullaby' was always playing on the radio and this consoled us. We would always write down how much money we needed to pay our bills and we always had enough.

I had no time for dating and was considering going into a relationship with a past boyfriend who had been calling me. He was married, but had started divorce proceedings and suggested we see each other again. He promised me he had changed over the years. I told God that if he wanted me to be with my man from Montana, he had better bring him to me now.

I was having a discussion with one of my friends about this one day, and I now realize that I was manifesting my soul mate, because I began to specify just what I wanted in a man: a tall man with blue eyes and brown hair, a stable man, in fact the man I had been dreaming of, my man from Montana. I still didn't know his name. I had asked the Creator time and time again, but had been told simply that he was my 'guy from Montana.' Little did I know that I was about to meet a man whose name was Guy Stibal. (Get it? 'Stibal' sounds like 'stable.')

The first time I met Guy was in June 1997, at a sweat lodge he was running. I had been invited to it by a mutual friend, Paul. I had never been to a sweat before and didn't know what to expect. When I drove up and got out of the car, I was struck by the similarity between the man who was preparing the sweat lodge and the man I had been dreaming about for years. This greatly piqued my interest, and during one of the breaks in the sweat I asked him where he was from. To my disappointment, Guy told me he was from Idaho. This confused me, but I still had a strange feeling about him. I figured that the universe was teasing me a little bit, since it does that from time to time.

When we went into Guy's house during another break, I had a vision of a picture I had painted hanging on his wall. There it was, a picture of a spirit guide, ethereally hanging above his dining-room table. I remember thinking, *How funny! This man is going to try to buy one of my paintings. I would never sell it to him. I wonder why he would try to buy it.* I disregarded this vision and went home.

My first experience with the sweat was admittedly a difficult one and I was glad to have it over. But this meeting with Guy was the start of a strange energy between us.

Guy

Six people showed up to the sweat lodge where I met Vianna, and apart from our mutual friend Paul, they were absolute greenhorns. I am sure that I cannot convey to you how difficult this is for anyone responsible for running a sweat lodge. Joe taught me that everything about the lodge, from the willows that made up its frame to the water that was poured on the rocks, had sacredness and symbolism tied to it. An understanding of this symbolism enriches the experiences one has in the lodge. Traditionally, an individual would grow up in a culture where this symbolism was an everyday part of their life. Since most of us did not grow up as traditional Native Americans, we must be taught this symbolism and how it relates to our lives, instead of it being a purely intuitive thing that flows through our blood. It is difficult to explain the sacredness of something to people when you are making them uncomfortable with hot steam, particularly if they have never experienced such a thing, while at the same time asking them to complete the ceremony should they feel up to it and permitting them to leave gracefully should they not feel up to it. You could explain the concepts, symbolism, and sacredness all day and they would still be likely to dislike you for pouring offerings of water on the rocks, unless they had the correct demeanor and understanding before they started, and the group that came with Vianna did not.

The sweat isn't for everyone. Some people don't do well with the heat, which is similar to that of a Turkish sweat bath. Some people become claustrophobic; others are afraid of the dark.

I kidded around with Vianna's group, doing my best to get them to relax, but after the first session of hot steam and prayer, Vianna calmly looked over at me and said, 'You are not having a spiritual experience, you are delusional from the heat.'

She was eyeing me with open distrust and skepticism, and I could feel her curiosity as she probed me to find out what I was about. I smiled at her remark and continued with the sweat, as Joe had trained me to do.

As the sweat progressed, I found that all the people there were having major problems in their lives, most of them due to relationships. (This included me, as I was separated from my wife at the time but not yet divorced.) There are four rounds to a sweat and by the end of the second round, the sadness and despair were so thick in the lodge you could have used them as batter for a cake. The lodge was stifling and devoid of oxygen, as it is at times when people bring strong negative emotions into it.

At the end of the fourth round, all the people had prayed, and I was about to close the ceremony when Vianna interrupted me, asking, 'Aren't you going to pray?' Her tone was challenging, so I obliged and said my piece.

When I had finished praying, I ended the ceremony so that the people could go home. They were obviously not getting much out of it. I think we were all happy to have the sweat over.

From that day, I couldn't stop thinking about Vianna. I would think about her every day. She had made several predictions in the lodge, and I took particular interest in the fact that her predictions for my life began to come true. I could sense that there was a strange poignancy about her, a deep and unquenchable sadness similar to what I was feeling at this time. This made me curious to see if she was awakened. For years, I had been asking myself when I would awake. I was unsure what this meant exactly, but I somehow knew that just maybe I had found someone else like me.

Please understand that Vianna was *spooky* in those early days. I noticed in the sweat that things would come out of her mouth, and it was as if there was another quality to her voice. Her readings were *alive* with the Law of Truth. The power you felt from her almost set your teeth on edge.

A few weeks later, I decided to go for a reading from her.

Vianna

Out of the blue, Guy came in for a reading. I remember looking into the waiting room and thinking, *What a good-looking man.* I didn't remember him at first, since I had already dismissed him from my mind as not being my man from Montana.

Bobbi took him into the reading room, and as I was walking up to him I felt that he was trying to figure out how to ask me out for a date. This amused me a little bit, but I didn't let it distract me from the reading. I gave him a good reading and sent him on his way.

Guy

When I went into the session with Vianna, I had been contemplating giving my ex-wife the house and all the money (what little there was of it), buying a camp trailer to live in and simply disappearing into ranch work. I felt despondent and worthless, but when I left, I was changed. I felt a power building in me as all the old resentments came up to be dealt with. I took charge of my life and didn't let my ex take advantage of me anymore. I got a divorce attorney and it was all over in a month. We split things up evenly, except that primary custody of Tyrel was given to Laura. I had deep reservations about her ability to handle the boy, but Vianna had told me that I would get him back from her eventually, though the road would be difficult.

I had written some poetry for Vianna as a gift for her earlier predictions and I left it with Bobbi, but Vianna followed me outside and asked me the meaning of the note. I told her it was simply a gift in return for her gift of prediction.

A week after the reading, I went to one of Vianna's classes, and she taught us how to do a body scan.

I was inexorably drawn to Vianna with a deep instinct that I could not define. She has the tendency to go barefoot, and this class was no exception. I complimented her on the shape of her feet, even going so far as to grasp one of them and caress it. This rather aggressive behavior was out of character for me. It confused and irritated Vianna and she drew away from my touch. She even attempted to hook me up with some of the women in the class. I was amused by her matchmaking, but it was Vianna I was after.

The group went out to dinner afterwards and Vianna was quite cool towards me during the meal. When we left the restaurant, I found that I had a flat tire on my old truck and Vianna asked me if I needed help, but I sent her home, thinking that she didn't like me.

Vianna

Guy's poetry made me very nervous, but it was when he came to the class that the energy began to escalate between us. I found him to be very handsome, but I couldn't understand why he would want to pursue a relationship with me since I had so many children to care for.

Guy was quite persistent. He sent me flowers with beautiful poems attached, and I began to vacillate between dating him and my old boyfriend.

Then my old boyfriend called and suggested that we have lunch together. We went down by Snake River with a couple of sandwiches because he only had 45 minutes for lunch. As we ate, he asked me to wait for him until he got a divorce. I was skeptical that he would actually get one, but I said, 'Okay, we'll see what happens.'

When we had finished lunch, we went back to my little jeep to talk. All at once, hundreds of bees started to swarm around the jeep. They crawled underneath the vinyl tarp coverings, and suddenly the inside of the jeep was full of bees.

Straightaway my gallant boyfriend abandoned me to the bees and ran back to his truck to save himself. At first my door was stuck and I couldn't get out. When I finally did get out, I ran to get into his truck with him, but he yelled at me, 'Get away! They arc following you!' and drove off.

In tears I walked back to my jeep. Most of the bees had now departed, leaving just a few that I coaxed outside.

The message from the bees was that my old boyfriend hadn't changed. I felt a little let down, but I knew the universe was trying to save me from a huge mistake. And yet I had just agreed to wait for him.

Guy

A few days went by and I began to feel that I had blown any chance I had with Vianna, when suddenly she called and invited Paul and me to a potluck dinner at her house. The thought of interacting with people made me nervous, but I had to see Vianna again.

When Paul and I got there, Vianna was going to the store and I jumped into the truck with her and rode along. I was acting flirtatiously — something I hadn't done in many years, if ever — but it seemed to make Vianna *very* uncomfortable.

It is always what is going on behind the scenes that is most important. What I didn't know at the time was that Vianna's children had made her promise not to date anyone for a while, since her marriage to Blake had been so difficult, and they took a dim view of me. Also, she was being courted from every direction. Her old boyfriend was asking her to wait for him, other men were asking her out, her ex-husband was still causing her problems, and there I was, right in the middle, without knowing about any of it. I had no idea that I had so much competition until weeks later.

I had brought some brook trout cooked with thyme that I had caught in West Creek in Montana, and the potluck guests seemed to like them. After the food, Vianna insisted that Paul and I sing the Native American song 'Cedar Smoke' for the guests. I wasn't really comfortable doing this, but I did it for Vianna.

I stayed until all the guests had gone, and I can still remember sitting talking to Vianna on the stairs. Around this time she began a 'come here, come here,' 'get away, get away' routine that lasted for weeks.

I began to ask around about Vianna. It was important to me that I didn't make another mistake of the heart, or because of hormones. If I was going to start dating someone, I didn't want to waste my time or make a fool of myself. The reports about Vianna were good and her reputation as a psychic was amazing. Most people held her in high regard, and she certainly fit the bill for the high priestess I was looking for.

It was at a second potluck at Vianna's house that we first kissed. That night we were unable to find any time alone until the end of the party, when I was helping Vianna put some chairs away in the garage. As we were leaving the garage, we were finally alone! The magnetism between us was incredible as our eyes locked and our lips parted for a kiss. Then suddenly Bobbi barged through the door, saying, 'What are you two doing?' We recoiled from one another, a little embarrassed at being caught in such an intimate act. We sheepishly went inside the house and I loitered around, waiting for everyone to go home so that I could have another opportunity.

That finally happened when Vianna and I met in the upstairs hallway. I couldn't help myself, I had to kiss her. When our lips came together, it was beyond physical attraction, it was as if we had been plugged into an energy source, a bolt of electricity that started at the top of our heads and went to our feet! There was a small explosion of light and we broke apart, both surprised.

What was even more surprising was that Vianna instantly slipped out of my arms and ran downstairs. When I followed her, she turned to me and said, 'You're on the rebound. You should go home.' She ushered me out the door and said goodnight.

Still dazed by the kiss, I felt very foolish as the door closed behind me and I took in a deep breath of crisp fall air.

I got in my old pickup and began the drive home, feeling an intense sense of loss. All the way I had strange feelings stirring inside me, ranging from enlightenment to anger, all in the same minute. I vowed not to call Vianna again, if that was the way she felt about me. But the strange energy of the kiss still lingered and I had to shake my head to rid myself of the incessant buzzing in my ears.

I called Vianna the next day and asked if I could help her clean up the mess from the potluck. She told me that it was okay to come over.

While we were cleaning, I noticed that she had a large amethyst geode in her house. I had studied geology and collected rocks as a boy, but I had never seen an amethyst as large as this. Later I found it weighed over 230 pounds. I found it to be a fascinating specimen. Vianna was complaining about how dusty it had become, how difficult it was to clean and how it needed to be cleansed of the energy of the person who had given it to her, so, since our relationship was *bright* and *shiny* with newness and I wanted to prove my undying love for Vianna, I picked it up and set it down outside so that she could wash it off with a garden hose.

Once she had done this, I offered to ritually cleanse it in a creek in the mountains to release the energy from its previous owner. With some apprehension Vianna agreed to temporarily part with her rather large treasure. Paul and I loaded it onto the back of my truck and I took off into the hills. We found the closest creek up toward Heise Hot Springs, and in a deep pool we let the water run over the geode for several minutes, as with a raised eyebrow Paul told me how ridiculous all of this was.

Vianna

By this time I was feeling more and more drawn to Guy. The next week, I invited him and Paul to a campout potluck in the mountains above Idaho Falls. As I was preparing for it, my mother called on the phone, heard Guy in the background and said, 'Vianna, that's your man from Montana.'

'No, Mom,' I told her, 'he's from Idaho. He can't be my man from Montana.'

My mother told me that that didn't matter, and he was nonetheless the man that I had been searching for.

Guy

The mountains were fine in those late summer days. The smell of pines and sagebrush was intoxicating. By this time, my divorce was final and I had lost my furniture, retirement money, and camping equipment, but gained a house, as Vianna had foretold in the lodge. I was starting over and it was good to be in the mountains.

Some 60 or more people showed up to the potluck and it was a fine time. We stayed up late and talked over the fire. The magic of the things that Vianna taught me that night healed my soul from the pain of my divorce. The stars were out, the campfire played on Vianna's face as we talked, and I was falling in love as never before.

The old house that I lived in was now silent and full of the feeling of divorce. The echoes of the past were loud in the empty rooms. I had parted with the furniture, dishes, and silverware. All I had was my antique guns, an old pickup, and my tools.

The one thing that hadn't changed yet was the sweat lodge, but that too was about to transform. When you get a divorce, people in your life generally make a choice: they either choose to be around you or they drift away from you. In the sweat circles I belonged to, some people thought that since I wasn't married to my Spanish–Navajo wife anymore, I shouldn't run a sweat lodge, while others felt that I was getting into a new relationship too fast and setting myself up for disaster.

While their concerns may not have been without some merit, Vianna and I were to beat the odds against us. During the next week I decided to send roses to her. These flowers were to have far-reaching effects. They were a symbol to others that I was serious. Vianna's ex-boyfriend was particularly alarmed. This was when Vianna made me aware of his presence – and of his displeasure.

Then Vianna decided to stage another potluck in the mountains. What I didn't know at the time was that this event was staged in part to 'feel me out.' Vianna was interested in me, but was unsure if I was indeed her 'man from Montana.'

It was a good thing that late summer was my only slack time on the ranch or Vianna and I wouldn't be together today because of my intense winter work schedule!

Again the mountains were beautiful this trip, full of the colors of fall. There was a crispness in the air, with the land breathlessly waiting for the onset of winter. I was enraptured with feelings for Vianna, but some of her associates were attempting to undermine our new relationship.

Vianna

I was talking to one of my girlfriends about Guy, telling her I wasn't going to date him because I needed to wait to get my life together. She took this as an opportunity to make a pass at him. She went to him and told him I wasn't interested in him.

When she told me what she'd said, I was upset. I knew she had hurt Guy's feelings, so I grabbed his hand and went for a walk with him up the hill behind the campsite. When we were in a private place on the top of a little knoll, he knelt on one knee and told me, 'I see you are a high-maintenance woman. If you will date me, I will cherish you. I will quit the ranch and change my job so that we can be together. I don't know what kind of life we can have, but I promise I will cherish you.'

I told him that I had given my word that I would wait until my old flame had his life in order. Guy sighed and, with an incredible sadness in his voice, said all was fair in love and war and that he wouldn't give up.

Guy

I knew her heart, you see. Across the distance of time we had met and known each other again. We each knew how the other felt, and the only things in our way were the pain we felt from past relationships and the people who wanted to keep us apart.

That night, as Vianna and I sat around the fire, I looked up to see the constellation Orion in the clear fall sky. I had been mystically pulled to these stars since I was a boy. They had special significance for me, as they did for Vianna, I later found out, but she hadn't been shown where they were in the night sky. I took her hand and showed her the belt of Orion, explaining the constellation to her and showing her the hunter with his sword hanging at his side. It was another of those special moments of connection that brought us even closer together. It seemed that at that moment we were truly in the center of the night sky with the constellation all about us, so close we could reach out and touch the stars themselves.

The Snake River canyon has some strange formations along its watercourse. Some of these have been the subject of speculation on the part of metaphysical writers, who have claimed that in a certain place there are doorways for spaceships. This was of interest to Kevin, one of Vianna's friends, and the next day he took us all up there. While we were there, I went exploring and found a tiny calcite crystal embedded in the rock wall. I used my knife to pry it free from the surrounding volcanic rock and handed it to Vianna. Apparently it was this little crystal that finally showed her that I was her true love.

This was the last day of the second potluck in the mountains, and we had fallen hopelessly in love.

Vianna

A few days later, Guy came to call at my home. We sat down on the couch and I asked him again where he was from. He told me he had been born in Montana and spent half the time in Idaho and the other half working the upper ranch in Montana. That's when I realized he was my man from Montana.

Had the Creator revealed to me who Guy was before this time, I think I wouldn't have fallen so deeply in love with him.

When Guy and I came together, I became a whole person. That was when my life began. It was also when the belief work began to come in. Guy was to become a partner with me on that journey, supporting me completely in the creation of ThetaHealing.

Chapter Eight

THE EARLY YEARS

Guy

When I got together with Vianna, what I didn't expect was the extracurricular agenda that God had planned out for me, and this included helping Vianna with ThetaHealing. Although I had wanted a great adventure, I had never expected it to be in the form of a healing modality.

I was one of the first people that Vianna used the DNA activation on at her offices at 17th Street in Idaho Falls in the late fall of 1997. At that time, she was exploring the activation and its constructs on different people in the classes she held. She would have people lie down on a massage table to witness the activation. When I had this done, it made me a little dizzy and gave me a strange feeling in my head. I got off the massage table and immediately sat down on the floor, slightly disoriented. It felt as though the top of my head suddenly had a hole in it.

Vianna came over and said to me, 'Your crown chakra is closed.' She reached down to the top of my head and grabbed the air just above it, then raised her hand a foot or so to open it as though to release fairy dust to the wind.

When she did this, I had the feeling that she was pulling part of my brain out of the top of my head, and then this was gone, to be replaced by a feeling of my senses branching out of the top of my head like the branches of a tree searching for light. It was a strange, intense feeling and I have never felt the same from that time.

I suspect that this experience opened me up to mystical essences I had been unable to connect to before then. There was something truly magical happening that fall of 1997. That time in my life will forever be a treasure to me. There was something so poignant about it all, so filled with the richness of true love, that it is indescribable.

My son Tyrel had thrown a fit when he and his mother had left and had become more than she could control. He moved back in with me and I was very happy about it, since it was another prediction of Vianna's coming true. Looking after him made it difficult for me to drive to Idaho Falls and see Vianna, however, so she started to drive out to see me. I was very tired that winter, doing my best to juggle work, being a daddy-mommy and having a relationship at the same time.

My mother and dad, God bless them, helped me with Tyrel all they could. He was admittedly a difficult child and wasn't doing at all well with the divorce. Vianna was very patient with him, even to the point of leaving her own children at night after work for a couple of hours all through that long winter of 1997–98. She called him her 'little wolf cub' from the time she watched him literally climb the walls in the old house and the trees that were outside in the yard. As a boy, he could crawl up any tree I had.

As for Andy, he was in and out of jail at this time and I was apprehensive about Vianna meeting him, thinking that she might be judgmental toward him. When she met him face to face, though, she liked him immediately and felt that he had a lot of potential. She told me that I had to wait for him to grow up.

During that winter Vianna and I began to make plans for our new life together. Since Tyrel was attached to the old house and grounds, we decided that we would take a loan out on the property and build an addition to the old place so that we could move in together. My intention was to get a steady job, possibly with the government or state. This was a very difficult decision for me, since I felt guilty about leaving my father and mother in a tough position. What I did know was that it would have been impossible to be married to both Stibal Ranch and Vianna, so I chose the latter.

I remember telling my father that I wanted to leave in March 1998. He didn't attempt to dissuade me, torn, I think, between wanting my help on the ranch and letting me follow my dreams. I also think he felt that I would come back at some point, having failed in my endeavor. All he said when I left was 'Don't forget us.'

It was around this time that Bobbi and Vianna began attempts to persuade me to teach seminars. This was about as far away from my plans as you could get. I remember them calling me up on the phone to talk about seminars one morning when I had just come in from feeding the cattle. I was unsure that I was the right person for the job, but I agreed to do the seminars until I found a means of gainful employment.

Vianna, God bless her, was optimistic. She was bubbly and full of life, happy to be healthy and with her man from Montana. Her reading sessions were increasing, as was the interest in her techniques. She told me that we would figure things out as we went along – a prospect that I found alarming – and I could collect the money, assist her in the classes, and do drumming at the end. With the greatest of trepidation, I agreed to go along with her.

Down from the Mountains and Off the Farm

When I left the ranch for the road I found that I was still rough around the edges. I was more used to talking to cattle than I was people.

Strangely, when I quit my job working for my parents, it was like going through a divorce. My parents and I had become dependent on one another, and for years after I quit the ranch I would feel the pang of loss. And it wasn't just my parents that I was leaving, it was the land as well. My family had been farming and ranching in Roberts since the 1890s. That place held memories in the very soil. You could almost hear the creak of horse-drawn equipment and the voices of your kin as you farmed the same land that they had. I had sweat blood for that land, just as they had. It was with very mixed feelings that I left it.

Meanwhile I had a hunger to do something extraordinary, but I didn't know how I was going to accomplish those lofty ambitions, or exactly what they might be.

Vianna

Guy and I dated through the fall and winter. He was there when Bobbi went into labor and stayed with me through the all-night vigil. When the baby was crying after her first medical check, he was the first to put his big hands on her. She stopped screaming and calmed down. We named her Jenaleighia Tray. She and Bobbi were to live with us for the next few years and it was an amazing experience watching her growing up. I realize that the Creator has always kept little children around me for motivation to move forward.

In the springtime of 1998 I was given the final validation that I was on the right path. At that time the massive box elder trees by Guy's house were in full bloom and hundreds of bees were gathering nectar from them. As I arrived for a visit one day, they began to swarm alarmingly around my little red car.

Guy was waiting on the porch, and I told him that I couldn't get out with the bees swarming as they were. He ran out, swept the bees off the side of the car, scooped me up in his arms and carried me into the house to shield me from the bees.

In the house, he calmed me down. I felt protected, and that is when I knew beyond a shadow of a doubt that Guy was the man who had the bravery to be in my life.

Guy

The stage was set. We took out a home-equity loan on the old house, and I quit my job to begin work on the construction of an addition. I planned to do as much of the work as I could since we needed to keep as much of the renovation money for bills and traveling as possible.

I had a basic understanding of building, but had never built an addition. It turned out to be a challenge. Take my advice: if your house is old, don't make an addition. Sell the dang thing and move into a larger, newer home.

I began to work at fever pitch because I wanted to complete the addition before winter hit. In the Snake River Valley, winter is always a practical consideration. It is winter that will crack foundations and destroy roofs and just about everything else. Snow is the great destroyer, yet the provider of the water that is in such short supply in summer. So concrete is poured in the late spring and the roof has to be up as soon as possible. After my friends had helped me with the framing and roof ledger plate, I was off and running. Concrete foundation, ledger plates, framing, window openings, roof beams (I was almost killed when a beam fell on me), rafters, roof boards, tar-paper, metal roofing, siding, window installation, endless caulking – and you have the basics once these endless tasks are done. This says nothing of the interior finishing. Then there is the need for openings to be cut into the house for doors, then the chores of insulation, sheet rock, plaster, painting, and wood finishing. This says nothing of the plumbing, flooring, and heating considerations. All of this was mine to finish before Vianna and her girls moved in, and I barely made it in time.

Our First Marriage, 1998

Guy

Vianna and I talked about just living together, but the desire for a deep commitment was too strong and I knew I had to honor her with marriage. We were married on November 11, 1998.

It was a cold night at the Monarch reception center, which Vianna and I had rented for the ceremony. We decided to do a handfasting ceremony conducted by a friend of ours, a minister named Ben. I told my parents that it would be a small get-together, since we had no idea how many people would show up. So when 200 people turned up to see the union with the man from Montana whom Vianna had dreamed about for years, my mother was a little put out. It didn't help matters when Vianna showed up late, mostly because a friend of hers was compulsively doing her makeup and hair. By that time, I was thinking Vianna had cold feet, my mother had visible storm clouds over her head, and my father was voicing his concerns over my marrying again.

When Vianna finally showed up, I don't think my family liked the eccentric Celtic ceremony either, but everybody else loved it. Vianna and I had our hands tied together, and at the end of the ceremony we jumped over a broomstick.

Then the reception started, which was a traditional potluck where everyone brought a dish. The smell of over 100 dishes was wafting through the room and our friends were wishing us well, but I am sure that my family was taking mental bets as to how long our marriage would last.

After the proceedings, we stood in line and greeted everyone, had cake, then stayed afterwards to clean up. Then we crawled into our over-decorated car and set off for our honeymoon, which consisted of a night at the Black Swan in Pocatello, a hotel that offered theme rooms. On the way we were stopped by the police for speeding, but the officer let us go since we were newlyweds. That is how we started our married life.

We made an agreement to renew our vows every three years for nine years. At the end of every three years we would have the opportunity to go our separate ways or renew our vows. At the end of nine years, we would have the opportunity to be married for life. As of 2010, we have been married a total of five times. At the end of the fourth time we were married for all time but missed the ritual every three years and decided to continue the tradition because we loved it so much. We wanted to be married in all the seasons and for all time. This was because our love has grown *with* us and not *away* from us.

Life in Roberts, Idaho

The Roberts area where Vianna and I came to live together is an eerie place. It has its own peculiar weather patterns, especially in fall and early winter, when the Snake River causes mist to form when the air cools down at night. For a psychic, this mist is a portal that makes it easy to see all kinds of phenomena. All sorts of people have seen strange sightings in the area, ranging from flying saucers to the ghosts of settlers and Native Americans dressed in ancient garb. Many Shoshone-Bannock tribes lived and wintered in the area. The road to the old farmstead that Vianna and I lived in is named Stibal Lane after my great-grandfather, who first settled there late in the 1800s, and people have seen specters of Native Americans in ancient clothing here. Legend has it that at the entrance to this lane there is a native burial ground. There were once many lakes and springs here, too, and because of the abundance of game, early settlers called this area the market, or Market Lake.

When Vianna and I started to live together, she began to tell me about all the terrible things that had happened in her life. She told me everything in an outpouring of emotion that lasted for the first two years we lived together – her past relationships, her childhood, her spiritual experiences... I know as much about Vianna as it is possible to know about someone else without living in their skin. The poignancy of her story was staggering to me. While not quite the horror story that I was to hear from some of her students later on, at the time it was emotionally challenging to hear the story of her past without being able to fix it. All I could do was listen with as much compassion as I could.

Being in a relationship with someone who is truly intuitive can be challenging, uplifting and downright perplexing all at the same time. Throughout my life I'd had my share of strange experiences, but these would pale into insignificance compared to what I would experience with Vianna. There have been times over the years when it has been strange just sleeping in the same bed with her, especially when she has been talking to 'councils' in her sleep. When we were first married, Vianna was getting a lot of spiritual and metaphysical information from these communions, and she would tell me a little about it the next morning. For the most part, I'd just sit back and listen to her with curiosity. The thing I couldn't predict was that I would unwittingly get pulled into these experiences.

One cold winter's night I was to find out just where Vianna was going in her sleep. That night I had a vivid dream. I was taken up with Vianna through what I can best describe as levels of illumination. We traveled through these lights until we were flying above a city that was made of what I can best describe as solidified light of different colors. We were taken to an open-air chamber, to what I somehow knew was the Council of Twelve.

The council members sat waiting behind a short wall of white iridescent marble in a semi-circle. As I watched, they seemed to shift back and forth between forms of light and human form. I found myself standing with Vianna in the center of the semi-circle as she calmly communed with these strange beings by using her thoughts in a vibration that I could hear with my ears.

As I gently floated beside her, I felt disjointed, as though I shouldn't be in this place with her. More than anything else I wanted to go back to connect with my body. My panic began to grow as the focus of the council turned to me. I felt their questioning presence in my mind as though I was a bug on a pin. They asked Vianna why I was there.

She said casually, 'Oh, you know Guy. I accidentally brought him with me.'

I began to panic as the council searched me with their thoughts. In an effort of will, I commanded myself back to my body. In a rush, my spirit became a ball of light and I was instantly tearing back through space and time to my body. I was to find that connecting to my body this quickly was a bad idea. Don't try this at home, kids, because the pain is intense! I felt as though I had run into a brick wall.

As I entered my space I found that I hadn't been breathing, though for how long, to this day I still don't know. What I do know is that when I came back into my body, I had to command it to breathe. At first my body didn't respond. I began to shake all over, then suddenly I took in a huge gulp of air as though I had been holding my breath underwater. I saw sparks out of the corner of my eyes as though I had been hit on the head.

For several minutes, I sat up in bed, taking deep breaths and feeling thankful to be alive. I looked over at Vianna, and she stirred and sleepily asked me what was wrong.

I must admit I was angry about the whole thing, since I had been minding my own business, peacefully sleeping, only to find that I had gone out of my body and had stopped breathing in the process. It was hard to articulate to Vianna just exactly what had happened to me, but she seemed to understand. Sleepily, she told me that I would be fine. Still angry, I told her *never* to do that again. Unconcerned, Vianna told me that she wouldn't, and to go to sleep. I lay back down, but all that night I kept one eye open, so that I didn't get pulled out of my body against my will.

On another night at about the same time, Vianna and I both found ourselves in a waking dream. We were in a room in front of a huge vanity mirror. I looked up and saw the Council of Twelve staring at us from inside the mirror, arranged in a semi-circle inside it. I asked Vianna what they wanted, and she told me that she had been talking to them for a while and not to be concerned. After a few seconds, the vision winked out and I fell into an uneasy sleep. Life with Vianna could definitely be unsettling.

Chapter Nine

TAKING THE TECHNIQUE TO THE WORLD

Vianna

Way back when Bobbi was pregnant and I was in the middle of divorcing Blake, the Creator had told me to take the information I was being given out into the world and to share it with others. I had felt as though my whole world was falling apart right before my eyes, and in the midst of all of this, there was the Creator telling me to take ThetaHealing to the world! But I also knew that God never asks you to do anything without providing a way for you to do it, and a way was found.

My first book on ThetaHealing, *Go Up and Seek God*, was compiled in 1997 and published in 1998, and I began to teach classes throughout the United States that year. The Creator was right: I would take the technique to the world.

This didn't mean it was easy. When I applied for my Q clearance to work at the government nuclear energy site outside Idaho Falls, I had to give every address I had ever had. When I thought about it, I found that I had moved 39 times before I met

Guy. So now I wasn't in a hurry to go traveling. In fact I was leery about travel, particularly air travel, and would have loved to have stayed at home with my new husband and my family. There was also the consideration that the younger children might suffer from our absences. But Guy and I took a chance because people wanted to learn what we had to teach.

Guy

I didn't fully understand the saying 'Truth is stranger than fiction' until I began to do seminars with Vianna. To this day I am amazed at the strange situations that develop when a metaphysical seminar is staged. Each seminar has been a mini-adventure of its own. In retrospect I can see that Vianna and I were being groomed with each class that we taught.

The way that the whole seminar thing started was via word of mouth. People would call Vianna's office and ask for a seminar, and Vianna would tell them that if they got 20 people together she would come and teach them. She kept focused on her original intention of waiting for people to ask her to come instead of joining a seminar circuit, and she always had plenty of students. At first we charged $200 per person and barely covered our expenses. It was discount hotels and cheap food.

Mountain Home, Arkansas, Spring 1998

The very first seminar that Vianna and I did together was in Mountain Home, Arkansas, of all places, right in the middle of the Bible Belt. In retrospect I can see that this shouldn't be surprising since Vianna's work can appeal to all religions, even those that can be fundamental.

We rented a car to drive to Mountain Home from the airport, and the winding road through the Ozarks made us both a little carsick. When we finally got to the hotel, there was a southern catfish competition going on in the lake by the town.

We went out to a local restaurant for dinner, but when the cheesecake dessert came all we could do was attempt to eat it. I say 'attempt,' because it was as hard as a rock. I was determined to take a bite out of it, though, so I finally managed to cut a portion of it off and put it in my mouth. It was dry and chewy. Vianna, meanwhile, was calling the waiter over and complaining to him. She finally had to call for the manager, who discovered that the waiter had given us the display cheesecake that had been sitting out for weeks. He apologized profusely and told us that he was sure that it wouldn't make me sick. It was hardly an auspicious beginning.

This first class was to be the foundation for the DNA 1 class. It was a two-day weekend course based upon the reading, the healing, and the DNA activation and its constructs. First Vianna would show people how to do a reading and healing. Then we would use a massage table to demonstrate the DNA activation. Vianna would have a person lie down on the massage table and put her hands on their head. Then she would have the other people in the class gather around and 'psychically watch' the DNA activation of the person on the table. Each person would have a turn until everyone had been activated. Then Vianna would train the class in how to activate the DNA in other people. This was to be the format of the classes for two years until piece by piece the belief work came to Vianna. The whole thing was designed to wake up the psychic abilities of the students. I once heard Vianna say that one day she would have trained so many people that there would be a psychic on every corner.

From that first seminar we were off on an adventure that was to grow into what people call ThetaHealing today. It would take a lot of traveling and not a little sacrifice, but we were somehow drawn ever onwards.

The Second Seminar, Santa Rosa, 1998

The second seminar that Vianna and I did together was held in Santa Rosa in the California hills.

The drive from Idaho to Northern California was a long one. When we arrived at the house where the seminar was to be held, we were a little tired.

Vianna went up to the registration table and attempted to introduce herself, but was curtly told by the hostess to go to the end of the line. She dutifully went to the end of the line and waited her turn to get to the registration table. When she reached the table she told the hostess, 'Hi, I am Vianna. I have come to teach your class.'

The lady looked at her in disbelief and said, 'You can't be Vianna! Vianna is 65 and has blonde hair.'

'Where did you get the idea that I had blonde hair?' Vianna asked. 'Look, I can prove that I am Vianna!'

She took out her driver's license to prove who she was. The lady looked aghast, but quickly recovered and welcomed her.

It seems that false rumors about Vianna's appearance had been circulated around California prior to our coming.

As it was, Vianna's appearance didn't seem to go down well. After she had been teaching for an hour the hostess and some of the students bustled her off to take off her blue jeans and hippie shirt and put a dress on her to make her more 'presentable.' Vianna took this pampering rather well, but inside I think it might have annoyed her a little, since she is more comfortable in jeans.

When the seminar was over, we began the long drive home. We decided to drive down the coastal highway, not realizing how truly desolate and how devoid of hotels it was.

Hours later, when we finally stopped at a hotel, Vianna opened her car door and had a raccoon crawl into the car right under her feet. It was as if it didn't see her at all. She had to remind it of her presence by telling it, 'Shoo! Scat! Get out of here!' Then it looked up at her with its beady little eyes and slowly backed out of the car.

This was my first experience of Vianna's odd incidents with animals. After that I began to notice that for some reason wild animals didn't seem to sense her presence and she had a way with horses and other domestic animals that was uncanny.

We left to find another hotel and it was late at night when we finally found one that was right on the beach. We fell asleep to the sound of waves crashing onto the California shore. Our second seminar was finally over.

It was in this seminar that we learned to cleanse ourselves at the end so that we didn't take any unfinished energy with us from the class.

Vianna

The first few classes were spent figuring out how to work with each other, and at first this was difficult. To begin with, the interaction that we had with each other in class was just as it would have been if we had been alone together. People would say that it was like watching a comedy team as we discussed things, flirted with each other and picked on each other.

Guy

Working with your wife isn't an easy thing, especially when she is the expert and you are not. You have to get control of your ego real quick or I can guarantee there will be a conflict of monstrous proportions. In addition, I understood that Vianna had been in difficult situations in her past relationships. This meant that she was adamant that such goings-on as male dominance weren't going to be part of the program either at work or at home. An inner voice said to me, 'Bend like a reed in the wind.' I had to do my best to let her steer the ship.

When I started working with her, I was also suffering from culture shock. Years of solitude had left me naïve. I just didn't know how to play the strange games that people play with one another. I felt useless, too – I couldn't type or use a computer, and this was what we needed. Viruses, e-mail, the internet, software, updates and all the other electronic appendages were a little overwhelming at first, until I realized that the whole thing could drive you insane if you let it. Eventually, however, I had to admit that computers, and particularly the internet, could bring nations together and create mutual understanding – if used correctly and with common sense.

Like many people who are self-employed, I created my job as I went along. In class, I immediately I saw the need for a manual for reference, so I knew that was something I could work on.

When we first started doing seminars, I wasn't a trusting soul. I found the world of the city (including, unfortunately, the metaphysical world) had its own unwritten rulebook of competition on all levels and I didn't like it. The real reason I stayed involved at first was simply to protect Vianna. I wanted to make sure that she was safe.

Vianna

We learned a great deal about people in our early classes. The first question that people would ask Guy was 'What do you do?' Some people thought that he was my gigolo and nothing more. Guy had enough self-esteem to ignore this kind of speculation and let me teach while he acted as my support team.

The fact that we were working together was completely outside most people's experience. For several years people were confused by a big man like Guy being involved in energy healing, particularly in our rather patriarchal area.

As we learned more about seminars we began to change our objectives, and our experiences improved. We realized that as a couple teaching classes we were under scrutiny constantly, and it was our honest humor that saw us through. People told us that if we ever decided to get out of teaching healing, we should become a comedy team.

We were with each other almost constantly, and after four or five seminars we had things down to some kind of science.

When the belief work came in, in 1999, the more belief work we did on each other, the easier it was for us to communicate with each other and with others. This improved our ability to set our boundaries properly, and we were able to feel great after the seminars instead of being drained by the teaching.

The more belief work that I did on myself, the less serious about myself I was, the more enveloped with the work I became, and the more humor came out in the classes.

I began to experiment with belief work in classes. Guy and I would work on our own beliefs, sometimes in front of the whole class. We soon realized that we had been in very difficult relationships and if we had changed our beliefs much earlier, things would have been different in our lives, as would our choices. What was comical was that the people in the classes thought that these early belief-work sessions between Guy and me were somehow staged beforehand. Nothing could have been further from the truth.

It was through Guy that I found out that it wasn't a good idea to remove and replace hundreds of beliefs in one sitting without finding the bottom belief first, because he developed flu-like symptoms from one long session that we had. This led to the digging work. With digging for the bottom belief, thousands of beliefs can be replaced in one session.

It was through the belief work that I realized that I didn't know how to receive and accept love. Teaching myself to receive love meant that I got along with Guy 100 per cent better. I also realized that the people I had married before had actually loved me in their own way, it was just that I hadn't known how to receive love from them.

When we changed our beliefs, Guy and I found we were no longer struggling to understand each other, and we began to enjoy our life together much more.

Chapter Ten

VIANNA'S LABYRINTH

Guy

The idea for Vianna's labyrinth came in the year 2000 when Vianna and I were teaching one of the early ThetaHealing classes in San Francisco, California. One of the ladies in the class asked us to come and have dinner at her house, along with several other people she was involved with in the metaphysical world. Her house was incredibly beautiful, or at least I found it to be so. It was set on the top of a hill; much of it consisted of glass, wood, and stone; and it was open and spacious in the California style. At the back was a labyrinth. It consisted of asphalt paving making up a left-handed labyrinth. (This means that the opening is on the left and the spiral path flows clockwise first and last.) It enchanted Vianna. She asked if I could build her one just like it. A little pompously, I said I could build an even better one. I wanted to demonstrate my undying love for my wife, and building a labyrinth was a fine opportunity to bedazzle her.

I had been studying alchemy and sacred geometry for some time and understood the labyrinth to be a symbol of a sacred connection with nature, of the umbilical cord that leads us all back to the womb, that intense darkness of creation from which we are all born and to which we wish to return. It is a symbol of the male and the female aspects of creation that fuse to create the Philosopher's Stone. It was this consciousness, this power, that I wanted to create when I built the labyrinth for Vianna. I began it that same year.

When I had said that I would build an even better labyrinth, I had created a challenge for myself. The idea I had was to create a *living labyrinth,* using stone and plants. At first my plans were somewhat hazy, but I knew where I wanted the labyrinth to be. This was directly south of the house in the only spot that it would fit. It was actually a pasture that was covered with thick quack grass and weeds.

I don't know how many of you have experienced quack grass, but to get rid of it is almost impossible without herbicides or similarly nasty weedkillers. The first thing I did was to borrow my father's tractor and put on a spring tooth harrow. I used this to tear up the grass, hauling the roots of the quack grass into a pile so that I had clean earth to work with when I began to shovel out the labyrinth pattern.

I made the labyrinth pattern as big as it could possibly be given the confines of the space I had available. Another mistake! Had I made it much smaller I wouldn't have had to work quite so hard or so long.

It was when I began to make the spiral pattern that I started to wonder whether I had bitten off more than I could possibly chew. I used a shovel to create the winding pathway pattern and the small mounds that defined each circle of the labyrinth. When

I had finished this first stage, the width of the labyrinth was about 45 to 50 feet, and as you all know, the pathway of a labyrinth is circular. This meant that the inside area or pathways were incredibly long, stretching hundreds of feet.

At first I thought about making a simple turf labyrinth, just planting grass and letting it grow. In retrospect I can see that this course of action would have been the easiest but definitely not the most powerful, nor the most beautiful, and I knew that I would be constantly fighting the weeds even if the grass took over the whole landscape.

I was searching for an answer to this dilemma when I spied some flagstones I had recently hauled from the Centennial Valley in order to make a path under the windows of the house. I had been visiting my parents and had stopped at a gravel pit to pick up some of the stone that had been deposited there. It was beautiful, with yellow and purple colors running through it. It seems that the Bureau of Land Management had left it there and it had come from a defunct gold mine. The different colors in it were attributed to the high incidence of gold and platinum; it was essentially gold ore. Energetically speaking, this made it extremely attractive to me. Not everyone can walk on a path made of gold, and I wanted Vianna to walk on a path lined with it!

Out of curiosity, I took the flagstones out to the labyrinth and laid them down in the entrance. I liked the effect and so did Vianna. This was the beginning of what was to be over 40 tons of stone, laid mostly by hand.

At the time I was doing readings in the office and we needed this income, but we agreed that I would take time off from work when I could and would work on the labyrinth then. My father was good enough to lend me his dump truck so that I could go up to the Centennial Valley, some 80 miles away, for a load of rock. It soon became apparent that one load was not going to be enough, but I was seized with determination. Once the first stone was laid, the labyrinth had a life of its own. It demanded to be finished, and it demanded that the stone be brought to it.

For the next three years this is what I did in my spare time. I would go up to the gravel pit, pick up each flagstone by hand and load it on the back of my father's dump truck. Then I would bring it down and dump it by the labyrinth. Some of the stone had to be split with a hammer and chisel, since it was too thick. All of it had to be carried in by hand and placed onto the path and the sides of the mounds. From time to time, people would come and help me. Periodically, Vianna would come out to dance through the labyrinth in her bare feet and bring flowers and plants to put in it. As time went on, I planted hollyhocks all around the outside ring. This went on until finally I had finished the pathway.

It was during this stage of building the labyrinth that Vianna and I decided to renew our three-year marriage and use the labyrinth as the setting. We decided to do another Celtic handfasting ceremony. We invited a considerable number of people and some of our friends volunteered to participate in the ceremony. So we had a rehearsal.

I remember it was a hot day, dead still, with the sun beating mercilessly down as we walked into the labyrinth for the rehearsal. We were all dressed in our finery – beautiful, flowing Celtic robes. As Vianna came walking out, she raised her arms in a flowing motion, calling in the winds to cool us down. 'Come to me, come to me,' she said in a mystical voice and the wind began to blow strongly through the black willow trees. Then Vianna told it to calm down a little bit and directed it to her liking with motions of her hands. I must admit it was a little eerie to watch.

We had music for the opening part of the ceremony and we all filed into the labyrinth, going round and round until eventually everyone was in the confines of the circle. We had 35 or 40 people with us. The atmosphere was charged with the power of the ceremony. Our friends Sarah and Ben acted as the priest and priestess, standing in the center of the labyrinth to direct the ceremony and to marry us, while Chrissie, Shaun, Eric, and Nini were stationed at each of the cardinal directions to invoke power from that direction. Vianna and I gave our offerings to each other, and when the ceremony was finished, we all filed out of the labyrinth, following the pathways out to the food waiting inside the house. For hours after the ceremony I was riding on a natural high.

I was still dissatisfied with the overall effect of the labyrinth, however, so I went to the mountains for more stone to fill in the raised mounds that defined the rings.

At the end of three summers of building, I took Vianna out and gave her the last stone to put in place. I was never so glad to see anything finished in all my life. The crowning touch was a spiral of round river rocks placed around the outside edge of the labyrinth. There were also small standing stones terminating each pathway, entrance stones on either side of the opening, and a stone altar in the center for offerings. I'm almost certain that Vianna spent $4,000 on plants, not to mention all of the plants I dug up and transplanted. But finally, in 2003, the living labyrinth was complete.

Once the last stone had been set in place, a strange kind of power emanated from the labyrinth. The air around it seemed to shimmer like a mirage. It was particularly eerie at night. You could see the spirits of men and women walking in and out of it and catch glimpses of strange tiny creatures out of the corners of your eyes. In the summer, hummingbirds found a home there and particularly loved the ring of hollyhocks that I had planted around it. They would come and fly through your hair, chattering in their annoyance at your intrusion into their sacred world. Winter, spring, summer or fall, the labyrinth was truly a magical place, but as you know, magic can create as many strange situations as good ones. I believe that because I created a *living labyrinth*, it became a center of power, a vortex that could change consciousness, manifest things and span the gulf between worlds. It became a home for special spirits and energies, a sanctuary, a center for magic.

The open doorway of the labyrinth pointed toward our little house and I believe that this opened a doorway into the planes of existence. You see, I had built the labyrinth with seven pathways to represent the Seven Planes of Existence and the All That Is essence that Vianna talked about. I had also done my best to infuse it with the sacred alchemy that would create power. With the gold in the stone, I had placed the essence of fire there, for gold is believed to be the essence of golden light from the sun that has solidified in the earth. The plants brought the essence of the sacred tree, the *axis mundi*. The labyrinth represented a womb and the umbilical cord of creation. The eight standing stones represented the wheel of the year, and four of the stones represented the four cardinal directions. The left-handed labyrinth path ran first clockwise, like the rotation of the earth around the sun, then, like the sun around the galaxy, it led counterclockwise, then ran back clockwise again. So the labyrinth was a tiny universe of its own, a microcosm of a larger one.

What I came to realize was that a labyrinth is in no way a linear or scientific concept but rather a mystical, intuitive one. It transcends anything that our rational intellect can comfortably comprehend. It is even beyond emotions in the normal sense. There were times when I was standing in the center of that place that I felt emotions that cannot be described, and perhaps it is best so. Whenever someone creates a labyrinth, they give birth to a living thing with its own personality and power. The more stone and plants I put into Vianna's labyrinth, the more it would *pulse* with a life of its own. It would literally *sing* with life, as the bright sunlight would awaken the hollyhocks planted around the outside.

People were drawn to walk the labyrinth for the peace and healing it provided. I believe that it was due to this labyrinth, at least in part, that ThetaHealing became what it is now, but I cannot explain exactly why. Perhaps it opened a doorway.

We held our third marriage there on a windswept moonlit night with just Bobbi and Brandy attending. It was the summer solstice 2004. That was our marriage for summer.

Chapter Eleven

THE EICHINGER PLACE

I call the Eichinger place the birthplace of ThetaHealing because Vianna's labyrinth was built there, and much of the information about the seven planes, the Road Map to Creation and the early belief work, began to crystallize while we lived there. In fact, it was in the addition that I made that Vianna had one of her most treasured visions of initiation.

Nonetheless, in many ways the old place became a prison that both Vianna and I had to be freed from. The old house itself needed all kinds of renovations just to make it livable. I did these renovations in between traveling with Vianna to places like Arkansas, California, and later to other countries, and I didn't get much sleep in this insane juggling act of seminars and building.

Unfortunately, the renovation job was never done. As much as I had come to love that old house, I would have done better to put a match to it and watch it burn, then build a new house among the ashes. That would have been easier and more economical, on many levels, including those that pertained to our health. The water was poor, and we had to put in a filtration system. The house was always cold, so we put heaters in each room, since a central heating system wasn't practical. The siding was old, so this was replaced. The carpets all needed to be torn out and replaced, the interior needed painting, and the kitchen needed to be remodeled, as did the bathroom. The windows needed replacing and I built a new porch. We even had a little garage built at the front. Still, the place wasn't good enough for the more 'sophisticated' students who came to visit us and told Vianna to move out! And all this was going on as I was making knives and drums for sale (from scratch, I might add), writing the first ThetaHealing manuals and books, and building the labyrinth outside the house, with its tons of gold ore as flagstones.

Also, I know it sounds odd, but I swear to you there is an intelligent race of mice living on that old Eichinger place in Roberts. I had been dealing with these pesky little infiltrators for some years before Vianna and I met. We came to call them the mice of Nimh from the Disney movie. These mice could find an opening into anything. Cars, the house, my shop – nothing was beyond them. They would attempt to eat anything that resembled food, even if it wasn't. I have seen them chew on old deer antlers, hides, and my knife-polishing compound. If there were no holes to be had, they would create them, even through aluminum siding. They would set up residence anywhere, even in the upper parts of trees. I poisoned them, trapped them, you name it. I took the battle outside and still had no permanent luck. In all the time I spent plugging holes in that old place (and I spent a lot of time at this), I never did completely stop them from finding a way into the basement.

Our car, a Volkswagen Jetta, became the home of a colony of the magical mice of Nimh. First we attempted to put psychic blocks up around the car, to no avail. Then we put poison in the car, but the mice stuffed the opening to the box with chewed-up bits of rags so that the younger mice couldn't get to it and not a bit of poison was touched. Finally we decided to try an unconventional mode of attack: we lit aromatic sage in the car. This seemed to work, but when we took the car to be cleaned, the cleaners thought we smoked marijuana because of the smell!

We thought we'd taken care of the problem, only to find we had a new infestation. On two occasions, I took apart the front dashboard to clean out nests and caches of food that were stuffed in opportune nooks and crannies. Once, when we were on the way to a seminar in California with our friends Chrissie and Ben, Chrissie began to hear strange squealing noises above her head. At first we thought she was hearing spirits, but she insisted it sounded like mice. Finally, we stopped by a grain silo and investigated. Sure enough, whenever you touched the ceiling in a certain spot, a faint squealing could be heard. Ben and I found a Phillips screwdriver and took apart the ceiling cowling and lo and behold, out spilled pink wrinkled little baby mice, and soon after their mother as well. We found more mice under the seat. We deposited our little stowaways by the grain silo and put the cowling back on, all the time praying that there were no more mice in the car. Thankfully, we saw no more of them the rest of the trip.

Eventually Vianna asked God what to do. She was told to park the car in a different place, underneath a tree. We found out later that a huge great-horned owl roosted on a branch of this tree. Every morning Vianna would find strange little fur-balls just outside her car door. When she showed them to me, I knew that they were the regurgitated remains of mice from the old owl. We never had a problem with mice in the car again.

Vianna and the old owl had a strange connection. The owl scared some of the Native Americans who came to visit us, but it would swoop down and fly over Vianna's head when she walked to the house in the early evening, as if to let her know it was watching over her.

During this time, my main reason for staying in the house – my son – left to live with his mother again. She had been awarded primary custody of him, as is customary in Idaho, and there was little I could do. Tyrel began to run wild, call the man who lived with his mother Dad, and refuse any contact with me.

While I did everything to get him back short of a court order, this left the upstairs room vacant and we began renovations on it. Vianna decided to create a God room with representations from all the world religions in it. When she had finished, it was a magical place, with vines and statues everywhere.

The Eichinger place itself was magical, and for seven years Vianna and I fought the good fight with it and developed the techniques that were to become ThetaHealing.

Chapter Twelve

LEARNING FROM EXPERIENCE

I had wanted adventures, and seminars are adventures, each one having a personality all its own. This personality is developed by several factors, one of which is the host. It is an extremely challenging thing to organize one of these seminars. I should know – I've staged a good number of these things myself now.

In the early days, Vianna and I had a lot to learn. A costly lesson was when one of the hosts collected the money for us before we got to the seminar and afterwards brazenly told Vianna that there would be no money coming to us, as it was now all gone. Her own business was failing and the money was never paid. This was a hard lesson for Vianna. At the time, ThetaHealing was just blossoming, and these funds were crucial to the running of our little office. Our business almost went under because of this fiasco. Afterwards we made it a criterion that we collected our portion of the fees ourselves, and we had considerably fewer problems.

Vianna

We all learn from experience, developed by drawing on the events of our rich and varied past. This development must have a certain degree of forgiveness for ourselves and those who give us the gift of these experiences.

Our early seminars were certainly rich and varied, and some of the most stressful experiences involved staging a seminar at someone's house.

Atlanta, Georgia

Guy

We found Georgia to be a beautiful state full of pine forests. But when we did a class in Atlanta, we got our first taste of just how truly eccentric people could be.

This seminar was hosted by a lady in her home. Later we were to realize that this setup gives the hostess way too much latitude for weirdness.

When we got there we found that our hostess was a sex therapist. Vianna and I are somewhat conservative when it comes to the subject of sex, and this lady certainly brought up every issue that we had.

We had 17 people for the class and things went well until the end of the first day when our hostess was curious as to what astrological signs Vianna and I were. Vianna told her that she was a Capricorn, and I told her that I was an Aries.

'Really?' she said. 'I've never seen an Aries who was monogamous.'

Shocked, I flatly replied, 'You've just met your first one.'

As if to challenge this, she then offered to find a ride for Vianna to our hotel room and to put me in her hot tub to soak! As we both beat a hasty retreat to our hotel room, Vianna and I wondered just what we had gotten ourselves into.

That next day, our hostess greeted us in a mini-skirt and sat on the floor in front of the class. What soon became apparent to one and all was that she wasn't wearing any underwear.

That seminar definitely was, let us say, a little... different. We finished it as best we could and got out of there.

Cassadaga, Florida

Vianna

As an intuitive, I receive prophetic messages in more than one way. There are the messages that come out of the blue sky, falling from divinity into my head gently – or like a thunderbolt, as the case may be. The other kind is a manifested message, one that is at least in part created by me through a connection that is created by me. Both of these kinds of messages are useful, but the correct interpretation of them and the regard that you give them are both incredibly important. If I don't give proper acknowledgment to divine advice, I have a tendency to learn something the hard way. This was the case with the seminar that I did in Cassadaga, Florida.

A short while earlier, totally without thinking it through, I had made the statement to the universe: 'I can teach anywhere.' So now the universe had something to teach me.

I had an uneasy feeling about the class before I got there, but I went anyway, for obvious reasons. Guy and I also took Bobbi and Jenaleighia along so we could all go to Disneyland afterwards.

When we arrived, everything seemed fine. I had been told I would be teaching on a deck overlooking a beautiful lake, and Cassadaga, Florida, the oldest spiritual community in North America, is a wonderful place, full of psychics and energy healers. As we walked down the street, there seemed to be a sign upon every house advertising the intuitive who lived inside and what they did. Some spoke to the dead, some were palm readers, and others used the tarot for divination. Guy was fascinated with the place and delighted by some of the signs that promoted the psychics.

The second day we were there, however, we found the facilities that had been provided for us were somewhat less than we could have wished for. The 'deck overlooking a beautiful lake' – well, I must tell you that they don't have lakes in Florida, they have swamps with water in them! And within those swamps are alligators! And a 'deck overlooking a beautiful lake' might just be a dusty airplane hangar with a concrete floor and a view over a swamp filled with alligators...

Once I found out that there were gators in the lake, I forbade my granddaughter to play within a mile of the place. Oh, I understand that to a lot of people, Florida is beautiful. But to me, it is a flat swampy place, redeemed only by the sun and the beach.

Needless to say, Guy and I were concerned about the teaching arrangements. There were some very distinguished students in that class, too, and they were horrified that it was being handled in such a fashion. One lady was highly outspoken about the unsatisfactory state of affairs, particularly as one of the other ladies present was wearing a short dress without panties – yes, it was our hostess from the earlier seminar. I had to take her aside and tell her to comply with the unspoken dress code that most of the world followed, i.e., get her panties on immediately. At the first seminar I hadn't known how to handle things, but I was learning how to deal with strange situations.

It became so unbearably hot in the airplane hangar that I finally took the class outside and finished the seminar in the shade of a tree.

That seminar taught me that respect was vital. What I had to teach deserved respect and should be taught in a comfortable place. That's when I made two resolutions: to acknowledge this myself and not to waste my time on people who didn't respect the work.

Maui, Hawaii

Guy

The first time that Vianna and I went to Hawaii was in February 2000. We were invited to the island of Maui by one of Vianna's clients who wanted us to teach a class there.

When we stepped off the plane, the feeling in the air was heavy and full of life. We rented a car and began the drive up the most paradoxical road that I had ever seen in my life. I say 'paradoxical' because the road to Hana is the most serpentine, meandering, twisting, and beautiful road that most people will ever have the opportunity to undertake. It is supposed to be the most winding road in the world. Once you hit the base of the mountains, a straight and level stretch is a memory, and if you are the driver, so is your innocence.

First, the tourists who take this road are all silly by default, and this includes *you*. I say this because half of the tourists are driving at the speed limit (10–15mph) to enjoy the scenery. Ah yes, the scenery! For a nature lover, each bend in the road is a new revelation of Mother Nature's botanical bounty. But sightseeing on this well-traveled road is at best a perilous undertaking. The challenge is to find a safe place to stop to enjoy this wonderland without being run over by the person behind you, who will be either a tourist who wants to reach their destination and go to sleep or a local who has taken this route hundreds of times before. These are both dangerous individuals. Generally, the best way to tell the difference between them is the condition of their vehicle. The tourist will have a rental car that is shiny and new. The local will have a car that is dented and washed with the salt air of the Pacific. But both will drive within several inches of your car in an attempt to force you off the road. The best course of action in this predicament is to stay calm and enjoy the scenery until you see one of those rare turn-offs. At such time I advise you to get off the road as quickly as possible, keeping your arms and head inside. Do not curse the person passing you or shake your fist at them, as they may be the local doctor or, in the case of the tourist, a traveling sociopath. Stop and smell the flowers, become serene and centered, and know that you will be doing this for the next two and a half hours.

You will never know when a vehicle is coming from the other direction, by the way, and should this be a large white dump truck which shouldn't be permitted on this road at all, pull over and stop in the hope that you aren't flattened. Close your eyes until the dump truck has lumbered past, missing you by inches and slamming your mirror against your window and utterly destroying it. At this point be thankful to be alive, and don't expect the local truck driver to stop, *as there is no place to stop*. When you have reached your destination, just call your insurance company and report a hit and run.

You should know that the bridges are too narrow for two vehicles to pass. The locals will not be likely to yield to you on these bridges, or to pay any attention to the speed limit.

Should you meet up with a tourist in a bright and shiny rental car coming from Hana, this means that they are late for a plane, and there is no more dangerous creature spawned by darkness. My advice is to yield to them and politely wave as they pass.

Should you come upon a tourist couple who are fighting, know that they are particularly perilous. Once again, pull off the road and let them get *way* ahead of you.

One rule of thumb in this place: be polite to everyone. Everybody knows everybody, and you don't want to win the Stupidest Tourist of the Year award.

After two and a half hours of the most beautiful and harrowing drive of your life, you will reach the ethereal Hana. This was where we did our first class.

Before the class, we had two days to recover from the journey and enjoy the incredible ambiance of Hawaii. Maui is a gentle mother, and it is said that the burial place of the goddess Pele is on the island. We stayed at the Hana Bay House, which was nestled in the overgrowth of what was essentially a forest. You could lie on the couch on the porch and feel the trade winds caress your body. This was the perfect place for romance. Vianna and I danced in the living room to the songs from *Message in a Bottle* and I enjoyed watching Vianna eating her first papaya in that house. It still strikes me how innocent the two of us were at that time. If I could bottle the poignancy that comes up when I think of those days, I could sell it.

The morning of the seminar, Vianna was intuitively told to wear a bathing suit under her clothing and at lunchtime we figured out why, as some of the students decided to take a dip at the Red Sand Beach. This place was truly beautiful. The ocean sprayed upwards as it hit the reef that protected the almost land-locked little bay. The bay itself was like a whirlpool, with the water swirling around in endless circles. I dove into the swirl and found the waters to be like a bubble bath. It was an optional nude beach, and some of our students decided to throw off their clothes and jump into the water stark naked. This was a unique experience, and I soon realized why some of us should wear clothing!

On that trip we were able to see some of the other sights in Hana, including the Rattling Beach, where rounded rocks made a roaring noise as the incoming surf moved them endlessly back and forth. This was also the first time that I drank the coffee of the islands. I was forever enchanted by the rich flavor and by the ambiance of Hawaii.

Stewart, Florida

By 2000, when Vianna and I went to Stewart, we had been doing seminars for two years and each one had given us new insights and important rules of thumb to follow. This one was no exception.

It was a long flight out to Florida, and the universe saw fit to place a woman who was transporting a cat in the seat right behind Vianna. At that time, Vianna was allergic to cats, and as it was a full flight, the airline wouldn't move us to other seats. This incident made Vianna determined to find a way to heal from that allergy.

When we got to Florida, we found that one of the ladies taking our class had given us a house to stay in. She told us that there was already a young woman staying there. When I met this woman, she reminded me of someone I once knew, and even acted something like her, which unnerved me a little, because the person she reminded me of was, in my estimation, unstable. When the woman was around Vianna, she was okay, but when she was around me, it seemed as though she was holding back a wild fury. This confused me, and I did my best to be extra kind to her, but this only seemed to make things worse. There was an odd feverish light in her eyes and she acted as though she was going to explode at any second. This was particularly unnerving when she was chopping vegetables in the kitchen with a sharp knife.

When I saw how strongly I was affecting her, I tried to stay out of her way. I whispered to Vianna, 'What's going on?'

Vianna told me not to talk to the lady anymore and that she intended to give her a reading the next day to find out what it was all about.

That night the energy in the house seemed to be charged with electricity. Vianna and I decided to keep the door to our room locked, because the other woman had a room adjacent to ours.

In the middle of the night we both dreamed that we were being attacked by some kind of spirit. We were awakened from this nightmare by the crash of the bedside lamp flying through the air and shattering in pieces on the floor. We ducked under the covers as Vianna sent the spirit to the light, and we spent the remainder of the night with one eye open.

The next day, during the reading, the young woman confessed to Vianna that throughout the night she'd had thoughts of killing both of us, particularly me! She told Vianna that she had just been released from a mental ward after stabbing her husband in a domestic dispute. Apparently I looked like her husband, and every time I talked to her, she wanted to stab me, too. She apologized to Vianna for these thoughts.

Vianna told her that everything was okay and retreated to our room. When she told me what was going on, we agreed that this woman had either brought all kinds of ghosts to the place or some other kind of weird energy was afoot.

Later that day, when our housemate went out in her little jeep, tires squealing as she angrily peeled out of the driveway, Vianna and I took this as our cue to 'ghost out' of the place ourselves and beat a hasty retreat to the local Ramada Inn.

We later learned that the lady who owned the house had knowingly lodged us with a recently discharged mental patient. When Vianna asked her why she hadn't told us about the problems that the young woman was having, she apologized and told us that she was only trying to help the woman and meant us no harm.

That was how we learned that even with the best of intentions, people can get you into trouble, and you should always follow your instincts if they are telling you to lock your door.

Chapter Thirteen

STUDENTS AND TEACHERS

Vianna

By the end of 1999 I had done over 20,000 readings and healings. As time went on I received more information and I transcribed the book *Go Up and Work with God* in the year 2000. At this time, the DNA 1 class grew into what became known as DNA 2, a three-day class that encompassed the belief work, and I began teaching internationally when I went to Australia for the first time.

Many different kinds of people come to the classes. Some of them are close to God, while others are coming simply for their own amusement. It is fairly easy to tell what sort of people they are by listening to them talk for five minutes or so. Then you will know what kinds of issues they need to work on and whether they are there to learn or for a social game.

One of the very best ways to know the kind of students you have is to be silent and listen to them without them knowing who you are.

One day when I was on the way to one of my classes, I got into an elevator with two ladies who were discussing someone.

It soon became apparent that they were two of my students and they were talking about me.

One of the women asked, 'What kind of a person is she?'

The other woman replied, 'I hear that she is a nice person.'

I couldn't help myself. I turned to the ladies and said, 'I hear that she is interesting.'

They said, 'Really?'

The doors opened and as we were exiting, I turned to them and said, 'Really.'

Then I went into the room. They were surprised when I went up to teach the class.

Another instance was at the other end of the spectrum. Years before, God had told me to put frankincense on my students' feet to honor them for coming to the class. Frankincense was one of the most highly praised substances of the ancient world and is excellent for soothing and calming. So, in this act of love, I kneel in front of a person and anoint their feet with it. I am uncertain how many ThetaHealing teachers actually go on to use this micro-ceremony with their own students. You can bet that a fair number of them disregard this aspect of the teaching as being demeaning, but I have never found it to be so.

In one of my classes in California, I hadn't introduced myself when I began to put frankincense on my students' feet, and the first woman I knelt in front of immediately began to act like the Queen of Sheba, turning up her nose and giving me instructions as to how she wanted the frankincense put on her feet. Having no idea that I was her teacher, she was treating me like a slave.

I didn't tell her or anyone else in the class who I was, but just kept putting frankincense on their feet until I was finished. Then I went to the front of the class and introduced myself.

You could have knocked the 'Queen of Sheba' over with a feather. She immediately began to apologize for her behavior, saying, 'I didn't know who you were!' I couldn't help wondering if that was the way that she treated anyone she considered inferior to herself.

From that moment on, I told myself that I would do my best to be thankful for those who gave service to others.

As I related in *ThetaHealing*, it was while I was in Hawaii in 2001, on Oahu, that Pele, the goddess of Hawaii, came and said to me, 'Vianna, you know that you should only teach the *masters* who appreciate this work. You told the Creator that you'd teach anyone who needed it, but just because someone needs it doesn't mean they understand or appreciate it. Change your intention.'

That was when I realized that I was asking for the people who *needed* the work instead of the people who *were ready for* the work. From that time on I asked the Creator to send only the masters who would appreciate and accept the work. After that, the people who have come to the seminars have, for the most part, been ascended masters in human form who love and cherish the work.

The First Teachers' Seminar

Guy

We had been giving classes for ThetaHealing practitioners for about two years when Vianna staged the first teachers' seminar at Labelle, Idaho, at a place called Triple Creek in the late spring of 2000.

Teaching people to teach the work themselves didn't make any sense to some people close to Vianna. They thought it would have been better to have kept all the students for herself and not give anyone else the chance to teach the modality. This actually would have been the easiest route, both in terms of administration and otherwise. But Vianna had been told that she should train teachers to take the work forward, and that is exactly what she did.

Labelle is right in the middle of what used to be the largest cottonwood forest in the world. When we drove out there, Vianna said to me, 'This would be a good place to live. We will live out here someday.' This came true, since our present residence is only a few miles away, and each day as we drive home we pass the birthplace of the teachers' seminars.

The first seminar was admittedly difficult, since we had an overflow of people we had no idea were coming to the event and I had to scurry to get enough food to feed them all. This made us decide that we wouldn't try to feed people at a seminar like this again. My mother helped us with the baked goods, but you would be amazed at how much food people can eat if they put their minds to it!

The other drawback was that Triple Creek was hard to find, not to mention it was in a remote location and people had to drive each day to reach it.

As the class was in springtime, Vianna taught outside because we thought this would be a nice thing to do. But we soon found that the cottonwood trees were dripping their sap onto the students, making their hair sticky, and onto the metal chairs, making it difficult for the students to sit on them. We had borrowed the chairs from the local church, and they were covered in sap when we had finished.

So there were several things we learned from this first large event. One was that catering for a large group is difficult. Another was that teaching outside is not a good idea. And a final lesson was that people can get lost in places they are unfamiliar with. All common sense, but it's amazing how this can get overlooked when you are planning an event.

West Yellowstone, 2001–2004

It was the first teachers' seminar that made Vianna decide to stage the subsequent ones at one of her energetic homes, the small town of West Yellowstone at the gateway to the massive Yellowstone Park. For many years prior to this time, she would go to Yellowstone to meditate and center herself in times of great stress. She loved the geyser of Old Faithful and the buffalo, elk, and deer that roamed in the park. So she decided to stage the events at a large convention center in the middle of West Yellowstone.

It is strange, but most of Vianna's early teachers' seminars were held at volcanic hotspots of some kind – Yellowstone, Hawaii, and New Zealand. The only exception was Australia.

From 2001 to 2004 we staged teachers' seminars at the Holiday Inn in West Yellowstone. The students must have liked the idea of doing the classes there because we soon had over 100 people coming. There were plenty of affordable hotels, many places to eat, fun places to shop, and of course the opportunity to experience Yellowstone Park.

The drawback to doing the seminar in Yellowstone was it was so far away from our offices that you had to take your whole office with you. I can remember taking vanloads of materials up to West Yellowstone with me – manuals, books, registration forms, contracts, paper, copiers, and all the other things we needed. Those of you who think that staging seminars isn't hard work should just try it sometime. Preparation is all-important, or you will quickly feel like a juggler who has too many balls in the air at once.

Mammoth Hot Springs, Yellowstone Park

Vianna

It was after one of our teachers' seminars that Guy and I decided to take a trip up to Mammoth Hot Springs, deeper into Yellowstone Park. It was summer, and elk were taking advantage of the grass that had been planted in the grounds of the resort, finding it to be more palatable than the wild grasses elsewhere in the park. This worked out well for everyone, since the lawn-keepers didn't have to mow the grass. There was, however, the drawback of elk droppings on the lawn.

When we walked up to the cafeteria, a tourist who wasn't used to wild animals spooked one of the female elk that was lying down placidly chewing the cud. The elk charged towards me, rearing up on her hind legs for a leap as if she didn't see me. As her front hooves were coming down on my face, Guy stepped in front of me and charged the elk, waving his massive arms in a semi-circle and bellowing in a deep voice. He was fearless and I thought he would be trampled, but the terrified elk pivoted on her hind feet and changed direction, then rushed past us, barely missing me.

This didn't seem a big thing to Guy because he had been around animals his whole life, but to me it was validation that he would stand in the face of danger to protect me if need be.

Chapter Fourteen

MOVING FORWARD

ThetaHealing began to blossom, but by 2001 I was exhausting myself both seeing clients and teaching classes. I carried on, but in 2002, when I found I was booked a year and a half in advance for readings, I knew that Guy and I had to make some major decisions. We decided to focus more on teaching because that way we could reach more people.

Intuitive Anatomy

Many of my students wanted to be able to intuitively see into the body with more clarity, so in 2002 we developed a 'Psychic Anatomy' class. Then we found out that the term was already being used, so we called the class 'Intuitive Anatomy.'

The first class that we taught was almost a disaster. It was designed to show students what different diseases looked like and felt like in the body, and the feelings that might be attached to them. But when we looked at each system of the body, we brought up the beliefs and emotions that were locked into each one, and the students began to act out those emotions in class.

The mistake I made was that I didn't stop to do belief work on each system in this first class. I was so keen to give the students the vast amount of information that was locked in the body intuitive that I just focused on that and expected them to do the belief work after class. This plan didn't work well at all. So I made the discovery that you have to work on the emotions of each system so that they don't cause challenges. This changed how I structured the class.

The second Intuitive Anatomy class was a small one in the fall of 2002. Guy had gone to the mountains, so I was on my own. The students in the class were mostly women, but there were two men. Unfortunately, it seemed that several of the women wanted one of the men and actually began to fight over him in class! I had to calm down the catfight. I made everyone sit down and start working on their beliefs.

After that, the class became something of a psychic boot camp for the students. As they cleaned up each of the body's systems, they became more intuitive and freer of negative emotional components. This is when Intuitive Anatomy changed from being a class that taught people how to intuitively recognize the body's physical organs and the interaction between systems to a class of clearing the beliefs in each system.

The development of the Intuitive Anatomy class did not come easily. Each class that I taught seemed to bring up something new for me to work on, especially the lung day. The respiratory system had always been a problem for me. The manuals compiled by Guy went through many edits as new information was added with each class. Intestinal day brought up people's issues of abuse, and reproduction day brought up issues of birth and parents. But it was interesting to see how people changed and grew throughout the class. As they changed, I changed. And as I changed, I worked with Guy and we both benefited from the experiences.

In time, the students wanted to teach Intuitive Anatomy, so we created a teachers' class and a teachers' manual. I expected the participants to teach a part of the class in front of the other students so that I could gauge their grasp of the material and their teaching skills. Somehow, they always chose the system that they had the most issues with!

The first certification course was held on Kauai in the Hawaiian islands in 2005 and produced two special things: one was the poem at the front of this book and the other was a song that Guy created at my request, my special song of Atanaha – a word, vibration, and meaning that came to me to represent the energy of All That Is.

Intuitive Anatomy became one of the crown jewels of our classes at the time.

The Closing Prayer, Phoenix, Arizona

I have to admit there have been some strange instances in the classes I have taught, but in my occupation common sense is very important. It is always best to keep a clear perspective so that you don't become hysterical and create 'psychic phenomena' where there are none. Sometimes events might appear to be paranormal but aren't, and this is exactly what happened at a class in Phoenix, Arizona, in 2002.

I customarily lead the opening and closing prayer in my classes, the prayer that is offered as thanks to God. I have the students form a circle with their hands clasped, right hand over left hand, all the way around. This can be a moving moment for the students, but at the very end of the first class that I did in Phoenix, there was an additional *frisson* when suddenly the microphone I was using gave me an electric shock that began to travel around the circle, passing from hand to hand all the way around until it was broken by someone releasing their neighbor's hand.

It took me the next 30 minutes to convince the students that the shock wasn't created by me but by a surge in electricity from the microphone. To this day, some of those people still believe the shock came from me.

Although I have witnessed manifestations of all kinds of things, common sense should always be our best guide.

The New Life Experiment

Over the years, one of the things that has helped me the most has been the New Life Experiment. This was developed in 2003 after I had done a great deal of belief work and thought that I didn't have anything else to work on. I felt that I had reached a level of harmony and balance – but nothing could have been further from the truth.

One day I heard a chuckle and I was told to stop saying anything negative about myself and others or even thinking anything negative. I was not to use cuss words or express myself in any way that was negative. The Creator told me, 'Vianna, this means that you have to go a week without saying anything bad, critical or mean-spirited about anyone. Not one bad word about your spouse or yourself. Especially yourself. See if you can do it for a week and it will become apparent how much your cells are accustomed to receiving all that negative energy. Your cells have to be weaned off the negative messages that are sent to them and learn to function by receiving positive messages.'

I thought that this would be easy, but I was to find that it was not.

The first time I tried it, I became silent and morose for a few days and felt as though I was going to explode.

Finally Guy said to me, 'Okay, what's going on? Do you want a divorce or something?'

'No, what makes you say that?'

'Well, you've been particularly quiet lately – you haven't spoken to me for three days!'

That was when I explained what I was doing and why I had been so quiet and tense for the past few days.

My friend Sky found out about the process, and the three of us decided to try it out. We began to catch one another in acts of criticism towards ourselves and others.

At the end of a week, I found that the cells in my body were so starved from not receiving the negative messages that I had been feeding them for so long that I went out to my car and shut the door. I sat alone in silence for a moment and then I cut loose with every expletive I could think of. It was as though a floodgate of emotion had been loosed, and this convinced me of how much I was missing being critical. It also showed me how to become a better person so that I wasn't addicted to negativity.

When you do this process for a few days, you will see how much further you have to go in your personal development. It will become starkly apparent just how addicted you are to criticizing yourself and others. Three or four days into it you may feel as though you want to explode. This means that your cells aren't getting the messages that they are accustomed to receiving, and it is important to focus on retraining your body with messages of love. You may feel anger building up inside yourself, too. If this happens, you may have to do some belief work to get rid of it.

It is when you see just how critical you truly are that you start to take real responsibility for your life. Many of us don't know how critical we are about either ourselves or the people around us. But how can we truly succeed in life if we are critical about other people in order to feel better about ourselves? This is how the New Life Experiment alters our perceptions.

When you catch yourself using a negative statement, always cancel it. Better yet, catch yourself *before* you say it and choose a different thought. Send yourself the love and energy to change it with ease and grace to a positive statement and permit the Creator to teach you how to move forward.

The Rainbow Children's Course

Guy

This class for the psychic development of children of all ages was developed from classes that Vianna taught to children in Idaho Falls during the formative years of her teachings.

What we found was that young children had little or no problem with the exercises in the class, while the older students were challenged by them, just as they were challenged by the young children who attended the classes.

In 2004 we staged a Rainbow Children's Course in Santa Monica, California, and some celebrities attended. On the last day of the class, several of the children started to act like, well, children. They ran amok, made noise, and were generally a nuisance to those who wanted to listen to Vianna. Vianna even gave the microphone to one of the older children who had Asperger's and the child began to order the class around, much to Vianna's delight. There are times when Vianna teaches like a *heyoka*, which is a Native American term for medicine men and women who teach people things in a roundabout way with stories and a strange sense of humor.

In the middle of the class, a fire broke out in the hotel and we all had to leave the building. The children loved the fire truck and firefighters and watched them expectantly, hoping for more excitement.

When the class was over, Vianna and I went upstairs to rest, thinking the class was over, but not so! We received a telephone call from a teacher all in a dither about a lady who had gone into convulsions and couldn't leave the classroom. Vianna and I had to go down to find out what was going on. We found the cutest, most adorable African American woman declaring, 'I feel the spirit in me! I feel the Holy Spirit!' as her whole body shook with spasms, much to the alarm of our teachers and the hotel staff.

At Vianna's request, a paramedic who was in the room checked the wailing woman's blood sugar and blood pressure. When it was found that she was fine, Vianna instructed them to leave her alone. She remained composed and talked to the lady for a half-hour or so until she had calmed down. The lady eventually began to cry and thanked Vianna for the class that had brought the 'Holy Spirit' into her. She went home and Vianna recognized this episode as an old African Christian healing.

Sacrifice and the Instant Healing

Vianna and I had been doing seminars for almost six years when we began to notice that without fail something would go wrong directly before we left to teach a class. It seemed that some kind of 'sacrifice' would be made either by Vianna or me, but mostly by me. At first these sacrifices were relatively small matters – a broken article in the house, then a cut that dripped a little blood, a bruise here and there or a bump on the noggin – but as time went by, the accidents began to be more pronounced – and dangerous. Once, the day before we were going up to West Yellowstone to do a teachers' seminar, I was moving a glass panel and cut myself rather badly on the arm. It was a large painful cut and required stitching. It was then that Vianna knew without a doubt that something was terribly wrong in our little world and in our belief system.

It seemed that as long as there was a release of energy before the seminar, the seminar was a success. We began to suspect that on a subconscious level we were giving back to the universe for what we were about to receive in the way of abundance from the seminar.

Vianna wasn't immune to this strange phenomenon. Prior to teaching a seminar in Seattle, she tripped over our dog Maji's food bowl. She took a nasty fall and my heart was in my mouth as I picked her up and carried her into the house. When I set her down on the couch, I realized that her knee looked funny and was obviously dislocated. At first she was screaming in pain, but then she calmed herself down and went silent for 30 seconds or so. Then she nodded her head and looked at her finger, which was bent to one side, obviously broken. She put her hand over it and closed her eyes. When she opened her eyes and removed her hand, the finger was back to normal. She then rose to her feet and resumed her day without a limp, or any pain, or any further mishap.

After these two accidents we decided we had to do some belief-work sessions to find out what was going on. It was in this way that much of the belief work was formed – through practical experience.

We found that both of us felt the need to give an offering back to the universe for what we received from it. Once we had changed this belief system, Vianna made sure the problem was solved for good by making purchases directly before each seminar as an offering to the universe. These were always things we needed, and preferably purchased from small businesses that needed the money or, even better, from people who were in money trouble. Vianna also made sure that people who wanted to come to the classes but didn't have the money could come for free.

After this, there were no more accidents and the classes became more and more successful.

Healer Wars at the Teachers' Seminar

Vianna

We did many classes in Hawaii after that first one on Maui in 1999, and most were on the enchanting island of Kauai. Kauai is a special, gentle place. It has one of the highest rainfalls in the world and has the most beautiful mountains, rainforests, and beaches that you could ask for. However, the energy of the island will bring up any issues you might have.

There are many stories that could be told about our classes on Kauai, but I will tell one from an early teachers' seminar.

I had always had a strange connection to the ancient Polynesians because of a book that I had read years before about the Kahunas, the ancient healers of the Polynesian culture in the South Pacific, but I had a lot to learn about the modern-day Polynesians. I was a bit naïve when I first met Kauilani Kahalekai, a Polynesian woman who worked as a singer and presenter at the traditional Hawaiian party, the *luau*, that was held for tourists.

Polynesians can be a little irritated by outside healers who come to Hawaii to 'heal their islands.' They feel the islands heal the people, not the other way around, and that many of the visiting healers are condescending in their attitude toward both ancient and modern Polynesia. So when I first met Kauilani, I had this stigma to overcome. She was skeptical of me at first, but as she got to know me, she saw that I was genuine. The other Polynesians who came to feel me out at the classes also came to see that I sincerely intended to give ThetaHealing as a gift to those who wanted to use it and wasn't attempting to 'heal their islands.'

It took me several trips to Hawaii, but I finally persuaded some Polynesians that ThetaHealing was a good thing. Then I staged two seminars just for the Polynesians, one basic class and one teachers' class.

When we decided to do these seminars, I thought it would be a good opportunity to take along Tyrel, Josh, his children, and his third wife, Lindsey, so that Josh could help me with the seminars. Lindsey had always kept the children away from me for some reason and I thought that this trip would help to break the ice between us. She also expected me to support her and Josh financially so that Josh could stay at home and take care of the children, and I wanted to give Josh an opportunity to earn the money they wanted. Don't get me wrong – Josh knew how to work and was excited about doing seminars, but he always tried very hard to please the woman he was with.

I discovered that Lindsey was actually shy and a little phobic. She opened up a lot on this trip and I thought that we could be friends. I wanted her to experience the islands, and I also wanted to watch my grandchildren play on the beach. Perhaps the intention of making peace in my family magnified the events of the seminar that was to follow.

In some healing classes, there is that special individual who wants to be the center of attention and irritates the rest of the class to no end with their egotistical antics. In the early seminars, we came to call these people 'triggers.' It is as if God has granted such people the universal purpose of bringing up other people's issues. This teachers' class was no exception, as when it started we found that some of the outside healers the Polynesian healers were so irritated with were actually attending. This was a perfect manifestation designed to bring up every issue that the Polynesians had about what they termed 'haole-healers.'

I must admit, three of those healers were a little challenging, even to me. They felt the need to put their 'two cents' into everything that I said, without really saying anything other than they were self-important. One woman in particular kept annoying the whole class with her comments, including some that were of an inappropriate sexual nature.

I did my best to balance the energy of the class so that I didn't have a cultural healer war on my hands, but at the end of the second day, as Josh walked me back to the room, I turned to him and said, 'I wish I could tell that lady to shut up, but I know it wouldn't be appropriate for me to do so.'

You have to be careful what you ask for on the island of Kauai, as I was soon to find out.

To their credit, the Polynesians showed great restraint until the last day but one. But finally the woman pushed things too far, saying something to the effect that her healing touch gave men erections.

That was all the Polynesians were going to take. One of them got up in a fury of indignation, pointed to the healer and the two other women with her, and said, 'You, you, and you, *shut up*! I don't want to hear another sexual comment from you again! We didn't come here to hear you speak! Listen to our teacher and use the work! This class was for Polynesians to come and learn this work, not to listen to you run your mouths! Can't you see our teacher is tired? We came to listen to her, not to you!'

She sat down and then another Polynesian woman got up and entered the fray. 'That's right!' she said. 'You healers come from the mainland to heal our island. Well, our island heals us, and it doesn't need your help!'

Josh and I were both frozen in horror as the anger ripped through the room, followed by a shocked silence that you could have cut with a knife. I had lost control of my class and I didn't know how to regain it. Guy and Tyrel were away making certificates, so any hope of using Guy's strength in defusing the situation was lost.

Fortunately, Kauilani saved the day for us by getting up and bellowing, '*Aloooo-ha*! Everybody join hands and say *Alooo-ha*!' She began to sing a Polynesian song that calmed and saved my class, averting a cultural healer war. The whole class got up and joined hands and shared in the song, then they all sat down together and the Polynesians began to do belief and digging work on one another so that they could release their issues.

I was able to end the class without any hair-pulling, and the Polynesian healers got their class and the opportunity to publicly express how they felt, probably for the first time.

Guy

After 2004, Vianna decided to begin doing the teachers' classes in Idaho Falls at locations closer to home. We used many different convention rooms there until we found that it was more effective to build our own teaching center, where we work today.

Chapter Fifteen

MOVING VIANNA'S LABYRINTH

Guy

In 2004, a man named Wesley bought the land that surrounded our little renovated house in Roberts. Straightaway, Vianna told me that she could see that houses were going to be built in key locations that she pointed out to me.

We began to have problems with Wesley over land boundaries and right-of-way easements that went through our property. Disturbingly, he also started to make statements about building a 'housing development' around us.

One day he knocked on our door, saying that we could either sell our house or buy his fields from him for an exorbitant price. Vianna answered him straightaway by saying, 'No, thanks,' but it took him two hours to understand that we really weren't interested.

Then he moved some people into a mobile home directly behind us. This led me to close off his access (which I had every legal right to do), so he decided to build a road around us. In the process, he damaged one of our trees that hung over the road. I got angry, since to me my trees were untouchable, and to avoid further problems, I called the police. They made him repair the tree and clean up the mess, but this infuriated his wife. She stormed up to our front door, shaking with anger. I was paralyzed, completely out of my element, but Vianna came to the rescue by screaming right back at her before offering to heal her arthritis and walking her off our property.

I must admit, I was getting tight under the eyes after all these goings-on. I thought that I had two options, fight or give up, but Vianna gave me a different one: move.

Vianna

From the time that I began teaching internationally in 2000, I had been flying almost constantly. Over the next six years, I had continual challenges with the radiation, altitude changes, pesticides, bacteria, and poor oxygen onboard airplanes. Each time I got off a plane my breathing was a little worse than the last flight. The doctor put me on prednisone so that I could breathe while I was onboard, and the medication helped me with the flying, but I had to taper it off each time that I took it. Eventually I used it more often than I would have liked and gained a lot of weight – 70 pounds over a four-month period.

The place in Roberts didn't help, since it was an old farmhouse with years' worth of accumulated dust, molds, and chemicals that were almost impossible to clear no matter how many times we cleaned it. Although I was attached to the place because of its mystical qualities, by 2005 it was looking as though our time there was over, and I thought it would be a good idea to move to a newer house with considerably fewer toxins.

Guy

I told Vianna that I would only move if she could find a place that had more trees that I had now, and she said no problem.

Sadly, I realized that we had outgrown our little place. Vianna had attempted to erase the memories of my past marriage from the house and found this to be difficult. The water quality was a problem, as was the age of the house. For all of its mystic attributes, it had become a difficult place to live in. New houses were starting to spring up around us in exactly the places that Vianna had predicted, and the last reason for staying at the place had vanished. The peace was shattered. The solitude was gone.

We decided to move away and take with us all that we could.

A House of Light, a Forest of Life

In 2005, we moved to a house that emanated life and light. All the doors were made of glass and the layout was open and spacious. The main room was like a cathedral with Gothic windows. This place was made of solid wood finishings with a chimney of stone and mantles in the modern rustic style. There were six acres to the property, most of it wild forest of literally thousands of trees, and it was located in a cul-de-sac at the end of a long lane. It met the needs of both of us.

When Vianna walked into the house, she realized that the man who had lived there before had committed suicide there and was still around. His wife, who had sold us the property, had neglected to tell us about the suicide, but we had it confirmed to us afterwards by the neighbors. It was no problem for us, since we just sent him to the light.

Vianna and the girls had to clean the place for two days before we could move in, and it took me two weeks to bring over all of our possessions. In the process I had to clear 15 years' accumulation of my junk. My hide-stretching mess was the worst of it; truckload after truckload went to the local dump.

When everything else was moved out, I found I couldn't bear to leave the labyrinth behind. With winter coming, I began to move the stones to the new home. Our ThetaHealing coordinator Daniele Sordoni, Tyrel and I moved the stone onto trucks and dumped it at the site I had picked behind the new house.

As I stood looking at the Eichinger place for the last time, I was sad to the very core of my being. Much of my adult life had been tied to this place. I had built a sweat lodge here and taken it down, lost a family, built a new home, created a labyrinth and married Vianna in it twice, and helped to create ThetaHealing. I was moving farther and farther away from my parents, and melancholy swept over me as I stood there under those massive box elder trees. I knew every tree and plant on that place and loved them all, but it was time to let go. There were too many memories there. I took a deep breath and drove away.

Life is about growth, and in order to become a better person, we have to leave old habits and attachments behind. What is important is what we carry inside us, the wealth of past experiences and memories that make us who we are. We should honor these experiences, but the way should be relentlessly forward.

We put the house on the market and it didn't sell at first. In one last intuitive act, Vianna removed the blessing that the place had bestowed upon me as its caretaker. Then a buyer called us the next day.

The new house soon soothed my melancholy, since I didn't have much time for it.

Vianna and I married for the fourth time on the back porch of the new house on May Day 2007. It was a cold spring night and just the two of us were there. I laid rose petals over the blanket that we sat on to do the ceremony, and we shared Kosher wine and chocolate and renewed our vows to one another.

I started on the new labyrinth as soon as I could. I made the new mounds and began placing the stone, but it was not until 2011 that it was finished again. I had saved some of the seeds from the hollyhocks that grew around the old labyrinth and I planted them around the new one. They have since grown to a height of ten feet. As before, Vianna took great pleasure in planting beautiful flowers in the labyrinth and walking barefoot on gold. Now her labyrinth has finally been rebuilt, and I pray that it has as much power as the old.

It was in our first few years in this new home that *ThetaHealing*, *Advanced ThetaHealing*, and *ThetaHealing Diseases and Disorders* were written.

The next six years were to be the most challenging of our lives together. There was a storm brewing – the growing pains of ThetaHealing – and Vianna and I were standing at the center of the vortex.

Chapter Sixteen

THE SONG THAT HEALED THE HEART

Vianna

As well as the health challenges I was having around the time we moved into the new house, what was especially difficult was the situation between my husband and his son.

When Tyrel's mother convinced him to go and live with her and her boyfriend, he was 12 years old and impressionable. Both Guy and I did our best to get him to come home, but in Idaho once a child reaches a certain age they can choose which parent they want to live with.

It didn't take long before Tyrel was in trouble. Soon he was so out of control that his mother was screaming for us to take him back. He had gotten into drugs, largely because of his mother's boyfriend, who later committed suicide because of his habit.

Before this happened to us, when people brought me their problems concerning children on drugs, I was sympathetic, but always told them that it was impossible for me to heal someone who hadn't given verbal consent to be healed. It wasn't until I had this experience with Tyrel that I came to know exactly where they were coming from.

When we finally got him back, we put him in rehab and it was a huge financial drain on all of us. There was only one place that would take a child his age, and it charged $5,000 a month. We had to do more seminars to meet the cost. Then, when Tyrel got out of rehab, we had to take him with us to several seminars in order to keep an eye on him.

This situation was tough not only on me but also on Guy. I felt frustrated that I couldn't reach this child. Although it was difficult, Guy and I hung on to one another through this stressful time.

I was also feeling disappointed with some of my instructors and students. Perhaps I had unreasonable expectations of them (and of myself), but the more classes I taught, the more I saw that while people had good aspects to them, I didn't seem to be able to keep up with the negative ones, no matter how many techniques I developed. While there were people who undertook the work for self-development and enlightenment, others abused it in various ways for the age-old reasons – to make a quick buck, to gain acclaim, to wield power… Some people had twisted the work to meet their own ends, and this was very hard on my heart. I began to feel as though there was no reason to teach anymore and that I was wasting my time. From the beginning, people had asked me to teach what I had to offer, but I wasn't prepared for this kind of misuse of processes that were sacred to me.

The various aspects involved in the formation of a healing modality were also a strain. Someone always had a 'new class' for me to look at or was creating a 'new manual,' all using

ThetaHealing as a springboard. Then there were the 'new' modalities based on ThetaHealing, the majority of which were the same thing with the name changed or God taken out. There were almost constant offers to run my business for me – so many that I lost count. A recurring theme was an offer to create a ThetaHealing committee or board of directors comprised of people who wanted control but would supposedly give me 'the last say.' There were also offers of apprenticeships, mostly at my expense and only if the apprentice could come and live with me. Trust me, a little recognition will bring strange reactions from people who are interested in you. At that time it just seemed that everyone wanted something, everyone was looking for an angle.

There were people who were in need of healing, of course, and this was fine, but there were too many people for me to accommodate them all and still have a life, which was one of the reasons why I had trained practitioners in the first place. There was also the administration of my office to deal with, not to mention challenges with my children, particularly with Guy's son and my own.

These and other factors were very difficult both physically and emotionally, and I reached the point where I was thinking of just leaving and going to be with God. This world was becoming too harsh and cruel and I wasn't sure if I wanted to stay in it any longer. Even though I had the belief work, I didn't know how to clear the unbelievable sadness in my heart.

As I explained in *Advanced ThetaHealing*, by July 2006 I was feeling extremely fatigued, sad, and disheartened, and my chest began to hurt all the time. At first I began to do healings on my lungs, but then the Creator told me, 'It's not your lungs, it's your heart. You have congestive heart failure.'

In utter despair I cried, 'That's impossible! I'm too young to have heart failure!'

But the doctor confirmed my worst fear. 'You are going to try this medication,' he said, 'and see if it works. Don't worry, Vianna, if the medicine doesn't work, you are young. You are a good candidate for a heart transplant.'

I admired his honesty and directness, but I was distraught. I felt that I wouldn't be able to continue the healing work with someone else's heart. Guy was overwhelmed, too, because our world revolved around me teaching.

Just the thought of having my name on a donor recipient list was extremely difficult for me, let alone using the medication, but I took it just the same. There were so many things going on in my life just then that it was easiest to use it until I learned how to heal my heart. But as soon as I started taking it, I knew that it was too much for my body to handle. I became dizzy and had fainting spells.

A few days later, I had some musicians over to my house for dinner. Afterwards, they began to play for me. One of them played a magnificent Stradivarius viola and the music was full of melancholy.

Then the musicians asked me to sing the music that came from my heart. I said they probably didn't want to hear it because I was so sad, but I went up and connected to the Seventh Plane and began to sing in a mournful tone.

As I felt the sadness being lifted from me through the tone I was singing, I suddenly saw all the reasons for my unhappiness and my sickness: I was holding old sorrows in the molecules of my heart. I had always worked on my beliefs without thinking of setting my heart free from the ancient pain it was holding on to. At that moment I knew that what I had released was the combined frustration of ages of relentlessly attempting to wake people up to their divine natures, only to fail. I saw the devastation of centuries of attempts to connect people to God. Ages of war, battles, and the stupidity of humankind were released from my heart.

In the middle of releasing this energy I wanted to stop, but God told me, 'Keep going, Vianna, keep releasing it.'

I asked, 'Is this mine?'

God said, 'It doesn't matter, Vianna. It's there. Release it.'

When I had finished, I opened my eyes and I saw the people in the room were crying. You know, one of the most wonderful things about being human is that we have the ability to cry. In some ways, sadness is really a gift. It is something remarkable to be able to cry if you can use it as a release. I realized that I had been harboring too much grief over my associations with humankind, but now I could live without this attachment. The sadness in my heart had been replaced by joy.

This process had healed my heart, and had I tapered off the medication right then, I would have been fine. But I didn't have time to make an appointment with my doctor (as I tell all my students, don't stop taking the medicine unless told to do so by a doctor), and I had made a commitment to do an Intuitive Anatomy class in Italy. So once again I was on the wings of a prayer.

The Borgo di Tragliata, Rome

The class was held some miles outside Rome at a place that was, at least in some respects, the birthplace of the certification of ThetaHealing teachers in Italy. Daniele Sordoni had been developing ThetaHealing in Italy for some time, translating manuals and books as well as teaching classes, and had arranged for us to run courses at the Borgo di Tragliata, an ancient villa and farm that had been converted into a conference center, hotel, and restaurant.

We didn't stay there because Daniele felt (probably rightly) that the students wouldn't permit us to get any rest, so every day we took the 45-minute drive through Rome's traffic and smog into the country. That drive was always a bit challenging, because the traffic in Rome was a great moving vortex that flowed with a consciousness of its own. Motorcycles jetted between the cars, and the cars themselves missed each other by inches. The smog could be a little intense, and the drive can take on a roller-coaster quality. Needless to say, we always arrived a little shaky.

The Borgo di Tragliata was situated on two hills, one with the conference center and the other, more imposing one with the restaurant. It was a truly ancient place and a good one for the seminar in terms of positive energy, as are most secluded conference centers. The only thing it lacked was working air-conditioning, so we were forced to open the windows to get at least some semblance of relief from the heat.

So there I was, teaching a new class in Mediterranean summer heat while suspecting that the medication that I using was causing more problems than it was helping. At times I could barely stand up. When I felt I was going to collapse completely, I would go to the bathroom and sit down on the floor until the episode passed. Then I would go back upstairs and carry on teaching the class. You know, in all the time that I was teaching that class, no one knew that I was having a reaction to the medication. What was ironic about the whole thing was that all the people in the class thought I was in the best health I had ever been in, and in a weird sort of way I really was in good health, because the Creator had already healed my heart.

Some amazing healings took place in that class. A beautiful lady had a large tumor disappear, and another had her diabetes healed. That was confirmed by her doctor. There were good things happening, but every time I took the medication, I would become sick. I went up and asked the Creator about it, and I was told that it was just too much for me. I knew that I couldn't go off it cold turkey, though, or I might have complications or even die. So I began to slowly lower the dosage.

As it turned out, I had to go home early from that class anyway because Guy's father was having a triple bypass operation and had a stroke. Since Daniele was a certified teacher of Intuitive Anatomy, I had him finish the last four days of the class while I flew back home. I cannot express how terrible I felt about doing this, and Guy felt the same way, but we felt that our first priority was to our family and the majority of the Italians were supportive of our decision to leave.

When we got home, we found that Charles had pulled through against terrible odds. It seems that the doctors had mistakenly taken him off the medication for his circulation, and when he had gone into surgery, this had caused him to have a stroke.

I had to go back to work doing healing appointments, so I didn't go to my doctor right away, as I had planned, but made an appointment with him.

Throughout this period, I kept having fainting spells with increased regularity. I would just *drop*, with no warning. The morning of my appointment I had a really bad spell in the garage. Guy had to bodily pick me up and take me to the doctor. My blood pressure was dangerously low, at 88 over 44, and that was when I was moving around. When I collapsed on the doctor in his office, I was rushed to the hospital.

Guy told the doctor he believed it was the medication that was to blame for my condition, and he was a little war-like about it. At the hospital they told me my kidneys were shutting down, but they thought that they would recover. At first, they didn't want to admit that it was because of the medicine.

A further complication was that my blood pressure dropped to about 55 over 33. I lay in the hospital bed, unable to move, while Guy screamed at the nurse and the blood-pressure machine went crazy. The little nurse was a trainee. She began to tap on the machine saying, 'It's never done this before.' Guy did his best to tell her that there was nothing wrong with the machine until finally she said, 'Oh, that's not good,' and ran to get the doctor.

As I lay there, I was completely overcome with fear. Some of you may recognize this particular kind of fear – the fear when you know that you are really screwed up.

I said to myself, 'Fine, take me. I'm coming home.'

Then I heard a little voice say to me, 'Oh no, Vianna, you're not going to die.'

Once the doctors had cleared all of the medicine out of my body and done an ultrasound scan, they found out that my heart was perfect. But then they told me that I was showing all the signs of being a diabetic. It seems that the medication had flipped me into diabetes. The doctors gave me insulin, saying that I would have to use it for the rest of my life.

The realization hit me: 'Oh, my Creator, I'm not going to die!'

The next day, the hospital sent me home with insulin and glucose. In two weeks, I no longer needed them. My heart and blood pressure were back to normal, and all of sudden the weight that I had gained over the years was just melting away. I would step on the scale and find I had lost three pounds every other night. I had started a diabetic diet because I felt I should, but then I started to eat whatever I wanted and I still lost the weight. In only two months I was 50 pounds lighter.

I think all this was in part because of finishing 12 years of doing the Creator's work. I heard a voice say to me, 'You have finished your nine years of indentured service and three years as a teacher. Now it is time for your divine timing.'

I wasn't sure what was going to happen next, but on some level I really think that I had a choice between dying or continuing to play, and I just decided to play.

Upon reflection I think that I had to release the belief 'I have to be dramatic.' I remember thinking, *I don't want to learn this way, I want to learn a smoother way. I don't want it to be difficult like this anymore.*

I remember the biggest fear I had when I was lying in my hospital bed was of leaving my husband. I realized that maybe I wasn't allowing him to love me completely.

In the past, I had always had physical challenges of one kind or another, and I guess I had always had it in the back of my mind that I was destined to die young. Now I realized that it was time to get that thought from my mind. I was here to *live*.

I knew the Creator wanted me to be happy, and I also listened to Guy when he said, 'It's not fair to die on somebody you truly love.'

This experience enabled me to treasure my time with my husband even more. However, I still have the comfort that the Creator is holding a place for me.

Chapter Seventeen

JAPAN

Guy

Japan has made an incredible contribution to the growth of ThetaHealing. Overcoming the language barrier is the key to starting a modality in a culture that is linguistically and philosophically so very different from the West, and we have been very fortunate in the Japanese people who have worked with us.

Megumi Okubo was the first person to begin teaching classes in Japan in 2003. She had taken a teachers' class in Australia and then started the not inconsiderable task of translating the early books into Japanese. Despite coming from a very traditional family, she is involved with the modality to this day and has written a book on the subject called *How to Work with ThetaHealing and the Unconscious Mind for True Happiness*.

In 2005, another Japanese woman, Hitomi, took the certification classes in Australia and continued translating the early books in correspondence with Megumi. Eventually she arranged for us to come and do a class to certify teachers in 2007.

The First Teachers' Seminar in Japan

The trip out to Japan was a bit strange in that we saved $1,000 by flying out to Denver, staying a night there, then flying out from Seattle to Japan. The plane had the typical scrunched seats, and I spent as much time as I could on my feet. After a nine-hour flight, we landed and went through Customs and into a brand new world that was to be our gateway to the East.

This was the first time that we had ever been to Japan, and for those of you who are considering going, I can say that the differences in culture and language are enormous. While the Wishton Hotel, where we held the class, was a nice place, we found the rooms were tiny and the beds were, well, shall we say rather solid to sleep on, at least to us westerners. After two nights bruising my ribs on this surface, I went searching for an answer at an adjoining shopping mall, where I purchased some lawn furniture cushions. I hauled them up to our room and after that I slept better, but I didn't know if I was justifiably missing the soft beds of America or if I was just a spoiled westerner.

We went shopping at the local supermarket for food and found that none of the produce was to be touched – you were required to use tongs or gloves to handle it. As for eating, I found that chopsticks made it fascinating fun.

We did our best to adjust to these cultural challenges and still be polite. We found that if you are polite, you will be taken care of by the Japanese people. This stems from their inherent compassion for others. If you plan to travel, you will find few places in the world as enchanting as Japan.

There were unfortunately a few issues regarding the financial and other arrangements for the course, mainly, I think, due to the fact that Hitomi was working towards a Ph.D. in some kind of alternative therapy in a school in Australia while still coordinating things in Japan. She was very intelligent and was a very good teacher. She taught some wonderful classes in India and helped ThetaHealing in Japan as best she could, but I think that she had more projects than she could possibly handle.

Nevertheless, the students were great, all of them taking to the technique with a lot of enthusiasm, and it was in Japan that I began to become more organized...

The Tengu – the Japanese Fairy Folk

Vianna

It was during the first teachers' class I ever did in Japan that I had a strange vision right in the middle of the class. Looking inside the brains of some of the Japanese students, I could intuitively see that they didn't work the same way as those of westerners. They seemed to be more analytical and ordered. I wondered why.

As the students were going through the exercise of going up to the Seventh Plane, I was asking myself what could have happened to the Japanese to make them so organized in their actions and thinking.

All of a sudden, I began to see a profusion of little people with long noses cavorting through the class, crawling all over the students. Telepathically, they began to tell me that it was because of them that the Japanese were so much more organized than other people. They pointed to their leader, a little person who materialized carrying a huge book. He looked at me with the most soulful eyes I had ever seen and told me, 'Okay, okay, it's my fault. I did it. I couldn't stand them not being organized.'

Off and on throughout the day these little people would blink in and out of the class, and I had to adjust to their rapid appearances and disappearances.

The next day as I was teaching the class, I looked over to see that one of the little people was swarming up Guy's body. Alarmed, I asked him what he was doing. He told me that he couldn't stand it, he had to make him more organized. He said he could make his brain work better. He began to reach inside Guy's head in an attempt to 'fix things.' I told him to stop it, but he ignored me and continued making the adjustments he felt were essential for Guy's continued well-being.

I walked up to Guy and told him that there was one of the little people 'making adjustments' in his head. He was dubious, but immediately after this, one of the Japanese students took a picture of Guy and brought it up to show him. There was an orb on his shoulder. Guy was not so disbelieving after that.

Strangely enough, Guy did start to become more organized afterwards and he seemed to suffer no ill effects from the ministrations of the Tengu.

Kyoto

Guy

Hitomi organized a trip to Kyoto for us after we had done the seminar. I had told her that we wanted to see some special places in Japan, though to be honest I hadn't meant that we wanted to traverse the length and breadth of the country! However, we were certainly seeing it – or rather, most of it. We drove all day in the hopes of seeing Mount Fujiyama, but alas, it was shrouded in cloud.

We were tired and a little carsick by the time we made our first stop. However, all was not lost! Our guide, Ukiah, had connected us with a Japanese sword-maker and a man who sold swords. First of all we stopped at the sword-seller's home and received a tour of his small workshop. I looked at many swords, but only one resonated with me and I bought it. It was mailed home to me and eventually arrived in good condition.

Then we went to meet the sword-maker. He was awesome. We watched a three-hour demonstration of forge-welding tamagane (raw iron) that was to become sword-steel. We all got to hit the metal in the first welding procedure and he showed us what went into making a real samurai sword. This experience was indeed a treasure.

The next morning we found another of those treasures that come along with each trip, and this time it was Ukiah's children, a little girl and two little boys. Vianna fell in love with them all, but it was the little girl who was the most loving creature we had ever seen. As we spent the day walking through temple after temple, she took it upon herself to take care of us and watched our every move to make sure that we were acting properly. We went to a traditional Japanese restaurant and, with Hitomi interpreting, the little girl schooled us as we ate the food in proper Japanese fashion. She was particularly horrified when I poured soy sauce on my bowl of sticky rice. Then we went to a temple complex that had tiny deer running wild in the grounds and the girl explained everything to us. She was a little confused, however, by the statues of 'starving monks' that we saw, stating, 'If God is abundance, why doesn't God feed those monks?'

We left Japan the next day, happy with our experience, and flew home.

Hero

Six months afterwards Hitomi decided to leave the coordinator's role and devote more time to healing, the art she was so talented at. When Vianna asked God what to do, she was told that she needed a hero to help her in Japan. Then she heard the song 'I Need a Hero' in her mind.

The same day, Hiroyuki Miyazaki, one of the students in the certification class, called us and began to talk to me about his concerns for ThetaHealing in Japan. When Vianna heard that he was on the phone, she insisted on talking to him, knowing that he was the hero that God had sent her. Hiro had never had any aspirations to become the representative for Japan, but he humbly accepted the post at Vianna's request.

Chapter Eighteen

THE DARK NIGHT...

Vianna

All my life it seems that my passage has been one of healing the past, particularly things that happened to me in my rather difficult childhood. When I was older and became more spiritually aware, I began to use belief work to cleanse myself of the pain of the past, even while dealing with the present. In this quest for self-repair I have used many means, from physical to psychological to, especially, psychic. I am not averse to using every means available to get the job done, even surgery if need be. To me, it is all healing.

One of the things which had been a challenge from childhood was the legacy of past injuries to my nose. When I was a little girl my nose had been repeatedly broken, causing me to have a deviated septum and smashed sinus on one side. This resulted in breathing problems later in life. You may not realize how delicate the structure of the nose is, but I can tell you that when something is wrong with it and with the sinuses, it is at best very irritating and at worst just *hurts*. By 2007 I had already had two operations on my septum and in my downtime between seminars that year I decided to have the problem fixed once and for all.

Once, in a class in New Zealand, I had seen a woman's nose heal before my eyes, but this was only after we had cleared her childhood issues with her father. I didn't want to go to that place in my own mind and open that Pandora's box. I had already done a great deal of work on childhood issues, but I knew that there were some terrible memories that I didn't want to deal with. I was afraid that full recall might change the way that I felt about life as I knew it. So I opted for surgery.

After I had scheduled it, one of the surgeons came home late from vacation and my surgery had to be moved back two weeks, which gave me less time to heal before the next seminar. I decided to go ahead anyway.

This surgery was to remove polyps as well as to straighten and restructure a sinus cavity. To do this they had to break my nose one last time. It goes without saying that the nose and sinuses are directly connected to the brain. When the nose is broken, there is the danger of an opening being made into the brain and infection getting through the 'barrier' of the bone. This was one of the major challenges in this surgery. Sharp instruments being used in close proximity to my brain was not an appealing prospect to me, nor was having my nose broken again, but I was looking forward to breathing normally and I was told that it was going to be a day surgery – in and out.

When I lay down for the surgery, I was suddenly terrified. I felt that I had reached a point of no return and I began to worry that I might not make it through. As the blackness of artificial sleep wrapped around me, I sent out a prayer that I would see my loved ones again.

The surgery took six hours to complete and when I woke up, it was to the most incredible pain that I had felt since my leg had been swollen all those years before. My whole head seemed to be on fire and even the smallest movement was impossible. I was given painkillers, but they barely took the edge off. An hour later, when I was discharged to the hotel room where Guy and I were staying, I looked like a mummy with my face all wrapped up in white bandages.

That night the pain got worse. It was so bad that it was impossible for me to do healings on my nose. I knew that something was wrong. We called the surgeon and he sent us to the emergency room at the local hospital. The doctor there told me that my pain wasn't being managed correctly and gave me oxycodone. When I took it, it actually introduced itself to me! It called itself 'Poc,' I presume after the writer Edgar Allan Poe. This was the first time that a form of medication had talked to me in this way.

Poe lessened the pain and I was able to start witnessing healings on my sinuses. Guy and I stayed at the hotel for two days, until it was time to take the packing out of my nose. When it was removed, blood came gushing out and shot across the room. This was obviously more blood than was normal. As the surgeon's assistant went to get the surgeon, I began to do healings on my nose and eventually the blood slowed to a trickle, much to the relief of everyone present. The surgeon gave me antibiotics, more Poe, and sent me home.

I only had a week and a half to recover before I was on the road again – to Australia.

Australia, October 2007

I went home to Idaho with a sense of foreboding. Those of you who travel will know that the flight to Australia is one of the longest in the world. I had been to Australia many times before to certify teachers, but I felt that this class was going to be different. It was going to be a large one, with over 100 people. Also, all that year I had been hearing rumblings about some of my more senior teachers in Australia. It seemed that one of them had been teaching something other than ThetaHealing – elements from other modalities that had nothing to do with what I taught.

I'd had trouble with this teacher before. Guy had wanted to let him go, but I had held off because I wanted to see the good in him and, possibly, bring it out. It has always been one of my aims to bring out the divine in others, and in myself. So I always held out the hope that this teacher would either correct his aberrant behavior or decide to leave ThetaHealing and move on in peace. Over time I had watched people who had begun to create mischief in ThetaHealing be removed from the modality one way or another, and I could feel that on an energetic level there was another clean-up campaign beginning.

I told very few people that I'd had reconstructive surgery prior to this Australian seminar because I dislike people's pity. As it was, I was challenged rather than pitied: several of the students decided that they would confront me on what they had been taught by the renegade teacher. One of these students said that as far as he was concerned, he could get people to accept any feelings or experiences he sent to them. He told me that he could 'download' anything that he wanted into anyone, without verbal permission. He swore that he could make them be anything he wanted and it would be for their own good.

I asked him, 'Who judges that?'

He said, 'I do.'

I said, 'Do you really think that you can make that kind of judgment for another person?'

He said, 'Yes.'

This was just silly, out-of-control egotism. Looking at him in the eye across the room, I said, 'If that is true, it means that I can download you with anything I want, as long as I think it is for your higher good, without asking you.'

He said, 'Yes, that's right.'

I said, 'Okay, I am going to download that you become a dog.' He laughed at this, but I continued seriously with, 'No, really, I think that it would be a good experience for you to become a dog.'

Suddenly he took me seriously and gasped, 'No!'

'What?' I said. 'Are you exercising your free agency? Now you know you can't live someone else's life for them. Free agency is a law of the universe. It defines us.'

I told him that I was sure that the purity of the Creator would not allow us to force someone to be what we wanted them to be.

He didn't seem to like the idea very much, but I think I got the message across.

The dissenters at this seminar had three main points to make. The first was that there was no God. They didn't like the idea of God at all. This had been an issue with a small number of students from the beginning and I had found that it stemmed from people's human concepts of God and from the dogma that was so pervading on the subject. This subject is discussed in greater depth in my book *Advanced ThetaHealing*.

The second issue was, as we have discussed, that of free will. This had also been a challenge to some students. I feel it is important to remember that when you are downloading or instilling beliefs from the Creator into someone, that person has to have *conscious acceptance* of each and every program that is given to them. For instance, I might know with every fiber of my being that my husband needs the belief program 'I know how to express myself' on every level, but I can't send a download of that program into him while I am in the other room and expect him to accept it on every level of his being. His unconscious mind is hardwired to reject such thought forms. To take another instance, a Theta practitioner cannot place one hand on a book of downloads and the other hand on a person's shoulder and ask them if they would like to accept all the programs in the book. The unconscious mind doesn't work like this. This is because of the Law of Free Will.

All of us have the choice to accept or ignore outside influences, whether they be thought-forms or the spoken word.

The third issue that was brought up at the Australian seminar was when would I be teaching DNA 3? For four years the DNA 3 information had been coming to me. I had been talking about teaching it and occasionally students would ask me about it, but given the argument I had just had over free agency and the way I felt about some of these people's behavior, I had no intention of ever teaching it, least of all to them. The words just came from my mouth: 'I will teach DNA 3 when I have raised someone from the dead or come back from a coma.'

At this juncture I must stress to the reader that it is imperative that we are careful about what we say, as it may manifest in our reality. This was a lesson I was about to learn in the most dramatic fashion.

Recertification, Los Angeles, California, November 2007

ThetaHealing had been growing as a modality since 1995, and by now I had a good number of teachers who had been certified as far back as the year 2000. Because of this I had decided to stage a recertification course to keep them up to speed on the new information that had come in. So it was that one week after Australia, I was in Los Angeles doing this class.

I wasn't properly rested and Guy wanted me to cancel, but I felt obliged to carry on. I felt terrible right up to the flight to California, but I had given my word that I would go and I was determined to see it through. Flying was very difficult for me because of the way that the pressurization and altitude affected my ears. My sinuses were still sore, and I knew that something wasn't right, but I couldn't put my finger on just what it was. I would do healings on my nose that would work for a while, but then it would begin to hurt again. Now I believe that the pain relief was masking a deeper problem.

It was good to see some of the old teachers at the recertification class, but it was a difficult class to teach from the standpoint of the emotional energy I felt coming from some of the students. Again I found that someone was teaching the work in their own way rather than as it had been given to them (and as they had agreed to teach it), and was even downloading the program that people didn't have to listen to me! From my perspective, ThetaHealing was something beautiful that had been created over many years through divine inspiration, and I felt very disappointed that this sort of thing was happening.

After this class I felt exhausted instead of uplifted, as I usually was after teaching, and I decided not to stage any more recertification courses for teachers. Once more I felt like giving up on the whole thing and going back to God.

The Dark Night of the Soul

I felt so terrible that I thought about cancelling the next seminar, which was in Rome the following week, but I always do my best to keep my word, so I went anyway.

As I got on the plane to Rome, a sense of foreboding washed over me, along with the feeling that I wouldn't see my home again. But I took heart and went forward – to face the greatest challenge I had ever had, one that would test my faith and reprioritize my world.

The trip to Europe was uneventful until the landing in Rome. The pressure change caused my ears to pop, and pain shot through my skull. I began to develop an earache that got worse and worse as time went on. It was the same kind of earache that I'd had as a small child.

When we got to the hotel, our room wasn't ready, so we went to the local mall with Daniele and his family, but the pain got so bad I had to have them take me back to the hotel to rest. I did a healing on myself and lay down to sleep the pain away. I can vaguely remember Guy trying to wake me up, but darkness was enveloping me. I somehow knew that if I kept falling into this darkness I might never wake up, and if I didn't wake up, I wouldn't be able to teach my class. That was my last thought as the darkness wrapped around me like a blanket and took away the pain. That was it.

Guy

I am not comfortable writing about this time in our life together. If I could, I would relegate this experience to the mental shelf of one of my darker nightmares, placed in a cage It could never escape from. To this day, I see it this way. To me, the shadows of darkness and the stench of death still pervade the memories of that time in the eternal city of Rome. But I know that others will gain insight from these experiences, and besides, I will write them down out of love.

I was at best dubious about the reconstructive surgery that Vianna wanted to have done to her smashed sinuses. This was undoubtedly the cause of the whole thing. I felt from the beginning that Vianna didn't have enough time to heal before she traveled, and I voiced my concerns about this on several occasions, both to the doctors and to her. But Vianna is the eternal optimist, and we went ahead with the thing.

The night after the operation, I knew things weren't right. She was in too much pain. Then there was too much blood when the packing was taken out, and the pain and discomfort persisted for weeks. I began to suspect that the doctors had botched the operation, and I still feel this way. I think that they opened several pathways for bacteria and viruses to get through the blood–brain barrier.

After the classes in Australia and California, Vianna was depressed, not her usual self at all. She was disillusioned, and what's more, she knew that something momentous was coming. I begged her to cancel the Rome trip, because I could see that she was tired and still in pain from the operation. But you see, Vianna has more courage than most men. She gets this from her connection to God.

I knew we were in deep trouble that night in Rome when she fell asleep with an earache, but then again, I had seen her heal from things like this before, so I hoped she would be up and about again in short order. All that night I kept waking her up to find out how she was doing, but as the night wore on, she became less and less responsive. Finally, close to morning, I began to get frightened, and tried to call Daniele to ask him to translate for me so that we could get her to the hospital. When I finally got through to him, Vianna was in a waking coma and was responding to me very slowly. I dressed her with difficulty and we rushed her to the hospital.

At the hospital, the doctor eventually told us that Vianna had some kind of meningitis and had to be transferred to the infectious-disease ward. Daniele and I were both given an antibiotic as a precaution. After that, we went to the infectious-disease ward and were informed that we couldn't see Vianna because she was in quarantine and in a coma. I could see her once a day only, and then only if I suited up.

All of this had taken up the whole day. As we drove back to the hotel, Daniele and I talked over the class that Vianna was supposed to teach. We spoke of Daniele teaching it, but thought that this was a bad idea, since he had never taken that class before.

Since I wasn't allowed to be with Vianna, I decided to teach it myself. I thought she would want that. I instructed Daniele to tell Vianna's students that she was under observation – which was true.

That night I called up Bobbi and told her the bad news. I also told her not to tell anyone anything until we had a better idea of what we were facing. I brushed up on the class I was going to be teaching and prepared myself.

I could feel the specter of death around me and around Vianna. I knew she was fighting for her life, alone in that hospital where most people didn't speak English. I asked myself, *If she woke up, how would they communicate? Would they be able to help her?*

The next day, teaching the class actually helped me. To this day, I can't remember much of it, but it was better than sitting doing nothing. Somehow news of Vianna's condition had been leaked out to the class, so my efforts at keeping the situation low-profile until we knew more were dashed, much to my irritation.

For the next three days there was no change in Vianna's condition. At the end of each day, Daniele drove me to the hospital, where I suited up for my fruitless visit. It was heartbreaking when Vianna was unresponsive. In one of the earlier visits, the attending nurse watched attentively as I attempted to get some response from Vianna. Then she walked over and began to briskly slap her face. Vianna responded with some grunts, but that was all. I wanted to respond to the nurse in my own way, but I didn't because of my fears for Vianna.

I left the quarantine room and leaned against the wall, then slowly slid to the floor and sat there in tears for a few minutes.

When I had composed myself, I questioned the doctors. I was told that if Vianna did survive, it was likely that she would suffer brain damage and hearing loss at the very least. There was no guarantee she was going to wake up in any case. She was given only a 50-50 chance of living, unless they found the right treatment. They were working on it with doctors overseas, as she had an American strain of the bacterial form of pneumococcal meningitis, so it had to have come from overseas or from the plane when we had come over.

On each of those three days, I left despondent, but I still got up the next day, taught the class, and did a good job. The nights in my hotel room were the worst, since I didn't have anything to deflect my mind from the dark, brooding thoughts that came, unbidden and unwanted. Those three tormented nights were the worst in my life.

Vianna

Suddenly I was in a strange place. I was sitting next to a man in a purple robe. His long hair was jet-black and he had a goatee. He was dressed as you might imagine someone would be from the time of Jesus. As we looked at one another, I could feel a musty, ancient evil emanating from him.

I gazed upwards to see a delicate light radiating inviting warmth.

The man followed my gaze and said, 'You know, I wouldn't go there if I were you.'

'Go where?'

He pointed to the beautiful light and said, 'The light. If you go there, you will lose yourself and become the light and you will be no more.'

I remember looking at him and suddenly hearing voices behind me whispering to me that he was lying.

Then out of nowhere I heard Guy's voice all around me, saying, 'Vianna, come back to me! Don't leave me all alone.'

I felt very disoriented and out of sorts, but I said to the evil creature, 'That's not true, but I'm not going to the light anyway. I'm going back.'

'You can't go back,' he told me, 'because if you do, you won't be able to see — you will be blind.'

'No, I won't!'

Undeterred, the man continued, 'You won't be able to see or hear and you won't be able to move your right arm and your right leg. You will be paralyzed.'

I heard the voices again: 'He's lying to you. Don't waver!'

Defiantly, I said, 'That's all a lie! I *will* have all my senses and I'll be fine.'

'No, Vianna,' said the evil man, 'you will die and there will be no way back to anywhere in the universe, especially back to Earth. You won't accomplish any of the goals you came here to achieve, because your time has run out.'

'I *will* go back,' I said, 'and stay as long as I want to, for there *is* no time. I can live 100 years and still have time. I *will* accomplish the goals that I have been given!'

This was when I came to the realization that I was out of my body and I needed to get back in it. I also knew I was speaking to a spirit worse than any I had yet encountered, and when I woke up I would send it to the light, the very light that was calling me home.

The comfort of that light had been my heart's desire when I first went into the coma, and now I felt an almost overwhelming desire to *become* the light. But once more I heard the voice of my beloved husband, with whom I had traveled on so many journeys, saying to me, 'Come back to me, Vianna, come back! Please don't leave me!' His voice was echoing, as though it was coming through a tunnel. I could feel my heart being pulled towards it. I was being pulled back to him.

I knew that somehow I had to find my body.

Then I heard a familiar voice calling to me and I was pulled through space and time to Bobbi in Idaho. I found myself in one of my office rooms, with Bobbi there rubbing my feet, saying, 'Come back to me, Momma.' She was saying this over and over again like a mantra.

My children have all rubbed my feet for me ever since they were small. When they were young, they used to have contests to see who could rub my feet the best. So in itself this wasn't an unusual thing, but what was peculiar about it was that when I was in Rome dreaming that Bobbi was rubbing my feet, that's exactly what she was doing in America. Apparently she had gone into one of the office rooms and imagined that she was rubbing my feet, saying, 'Come back to me, Momma, come back to me.'

That was when I found my body. I saw the top of my head and knew that I was going to make it back.

I began to push my soul into my body a little at a time. I did this several times, only to be sucked back out. I remember making it into my chest one time. I knew that if I could connect all the way down to my ankles, I would be back permanently. I made another attempt, giving myself a big head start, much as you would to start your momentum on a swing. I went in and out of my body five or six times like that, then I made one last effort and made it to my calves. Yet again I felt myself being pulled out, but then somehow I was rushing right into my body and I was there like a hand in a glove.

My body felt much smaller than I remembered. I felt it begin to grab me, and as it did so, I opened my eyes.

I was awake.

That was when the drama really began.

Waking from the Coma

When I first married Guy, one of the first things I told him was that if I ever went into a coma not to shut me off because I was coming back. On some level I knew this was an experience I was going to go through. I don't know everything there is to know, but I believe that the ultimate test of healing abilities is to bring the body back from a near-death experience. I imagine this experience releases the right chemicals for enlightenment on all levels – physical, mental, and emotional. So this was the ultimate test for me in this existence. It is definitely not for everyone, however.

I woke up in a stark yellow-colored room. It was night-time. I had no idea where I was, but I realized I was tied to a bed and completely naked under the sheets. I started screaming Guy's name.

The nurse on duty was frightened and called for someone, I assume the head nurse. He came in and had me squeeze his fingers. He asked me in broken English if I knew who I was. He didn't explain to me where I was or what was going on. I insisted he contact my husband, but he ignored me and began to test my responses. He asked me where I lived and how old I was. I felt the horror of wondering what had happened to me. I asked about the safety of my husband, thinking that I might have been in an accident with him. The attendant assured me that my husband was all right and I just had to wait until morning for the doctor to come in and see me.

After I had passed his tests, he walked out of the room with the young nurse. I watched the two of them talk for a few minutes just outside the doorway, then begin to kiss and caress each other. This only added to my sense of disorientation and dislocation.

Apparently the medical staff had put a catheter in me, and I had kept pulling it out while I was in the coma, which was one reason why they had tied me down. Now I attempted to get loose from the ties and the nurses screamed at me that I wasn't allowed to move, but due to the language barrier, they couldn't tell me why. For my part, I couldn't understand why they were talking some weird garbled Russian.

There was a loud pounding in my head, and for some reason it was accompanied by irritating organ music. This music wouldn't go away, and later I found out that it was barely audible music that was played in the hospital to help healing. No one seemed to be able to hear it but me and some housekeepers I later heard commenting on it. This music almost drove me insane, and I think that it was the other side that was calling to me.

From time to time that first night I could feel that I was once again close to the light that I had seen when I was in the coma. It was as if it was just an arm's length away and I could touch it if I wanted to. I was afraid to go to sleep, thinking that I wouldn't make it back again. So I lay there all night long, staring at the only thing with any definition in the room, which was a window. After a while I realized that the window wasn't to the outside world but to a hallway. This place was bigger than I had thought. I lay there waiting for morning and for Guy to come and rescue me.

Awake

When the doctor came to see me in the morning, he had a weird snappy demeanor. He asked me questions and ran me through tests in clipped English. I thought he was Russian.

He told me that I had a bacterium called *Neisseria meningitides* and my chances of recovery were now 50-50 for a full healing. None of this made any sense to me.

I begged him to call my husband, but he said, 'No phone calls. You have just come out of a coma and have to be isolated. I will not call your husband.'

I begged him, but he still refused.

Then I began to get annoyed. Thinking I was in Idaho, even though I was talking to Russians, I told him, 'If you don't let me call my husband, I will sue you!'

This amused him. He began to chuckle and said, 'Go right ahead. You can't sue me.'

I yelled at him but he ignored me and walked out of the room. Feeling deflated, I quieted down. I wondered how to get word to my husband.

The day passed slowly until another doctor examined me in the afternoon. He was nice to me and I noticed that he had big ears, like a buddha. I commented on this and asked him to call my husband. He said, 'Is this your number?' and showed me a number on his cell phone.

I said, 'No, that isn't my number,' and gave him my Idaho Falls number. I was still confused as to where I was.

Regardless, he went outside and called the number he had shown me. It was Daniele's number. He told Daniele that I was awake and that my husband could come and see me, but only for 30 minutes as before.

When Guy came to see me, all suited up like a spaceman, he told me where I was and what had happened to me. I felt devastated, but at the same time I was alive and I felt great, at least for the time being. I begged Guy to take me away with him, but the nurses told me that I had to stay and he had to leave.

At the end of the first day out of the coma, I remember looking at the IV bag in an attempt to read the label and find out what the contents were. It looked like a bag of minerals and I thought that some of them looked like things I was allergic to. So I pulled the IV out of my right arm.

Blood went squirting everywhere and the nurses ran screaming to me and wrapped up my arm. I told them that the IV in my left arm was messed up because I could see that the fluid from it was dripping onto a bandage that was strapped to my arm. They explained that this was so that the fluid could be absorbed into the skin of my left arm and not into my veins. This confused me and I kept trying to tell them that the IV was set up wrongly. I was so disoriented, but I knew that I was a healer, that I had children, and that I had to go home.

It was the next afternoon that the pain hit me. It was worse than anything I had ever experienced before. Every part of my body hurt.

The medical staff told me that they had given me an enormous amount of prednisone in an attempt to pull me out of the coma and this was one reason why I couldn't sleep and why they had me tied down: they were afraid that if I got up my heart would explode. They were shocked that I had woken up at all. They would only give me tiny sips of water and refused to let me drink 'excessively' for the next few days.

My body felt foreign to me, I think because I had gone without food for days and had had so little water. My hands were a yellow color and looked like bird's claws. It felt as though I was looking at someone else's arms and hands, not my own. Both of my arms were one solid bruise from top to bottom. This was due to the difficulty the nurses had finding veins and also because they were still using steel needles in Italy. A nurse told me that the appearance of my hands would never recover and I had phlebitis.

I had no feeling in my bowels or bladder and voided them without knowing that I had done so. When I filled up the catheter, I pulled it out. There was no buzzer to call the nurse and I cried out for help and thrashed around.

It was during this time that I was called all kinds of names by the nurses and attendants. They were very frustrated with the 'stupid American.' I had never been treated this way before. My experiences in Italy had all been positive up to that point.

One of the attendants even came into the room in the middle of the night, lifted up my sheet and told me not to be sad and that I had a beautiful body. I pulled the sheet around me in a panic and he left the room.

I fell asleep and woke up the next morning to another examination from the attending doctor. I was told that I would only have to go through three more days of antibiotics and then I could leave, but this turned out to be false.

Every day I woke to the same nightmare. One of the few things that kept me going at this time was mentally planning Bobbi's wedding the following summer. I was *not* going to miss her wedding. I was going to be *very* disappointed if I died before it.

I was still on the brink, however. At one point my blood pressure read 344 over 200, and the nurse told me that this was a correct reading. I argued that it had to be wrong because I didn't have a blood pressure cuff on, and added that if it was accurate, I would soon be dead. The nurse replied that death would be much better than where I was now. That's Italian hospital humor for you! I started crying.

One day the head of the hospital came to talk to me. He spoke perfect English. He told me he was going to send me down for a MRI scan. He said he didn't personally treat many people, but he would look into my case. I think this was because so many people had called the hospital out of concern for me.

I was dressed in some paper clothing and put into a wheelchair. When I left the room, the organ music stopped for the first time. I met Guy on the way to the scan and went bananas, yelling, 'Get me out of this place!' I was quickly wheeled off before I could make any more trouble. Guy followed on.

After the MRI scan, I found out I was being rolled back to the isolation room that I had been in for the last six days. That was it – I emphatically refused to go back. Guy told me to cooperate but, convinced that there was a conspiracy and I was in mortal danger, I told him no. I tried to stand up and escape, but Guy grabbed me and told me that I was going to cooperate. 'No!' I said, and hit him in the face as hard as I could, falling back into the wheelchair as I did so.

After that, they took me to a section of the hospital that was 'semi-quarantined.' For the first time Guy was allowed to come into my room without suiting up first. When he arrived, I told him that the place was awful, it was all a conspiracy against me and if I went back into quarantine they would kill me. It must have looked as though I'd gone crazy.

I asked Guy to take me right away to see a doctor upstairs, because we had an appointment to discuss my treatment. He didn't believe me. I became infuriated with him and hauled off and hit him twice in the face.

That was too much – Guy and the nurses held me down and gave me a sedative.

Apparently it is normal for people who survive meningitis to go through fits of rage, so the hospital staff was prepared for the way I acted, but I don't think Guy was.

Guy

I knew that Vianna had been through a terrible ordeal, but I was unsure just what was going on with her. After she hit me, it was decided that I would sleep in the same room as her to keep her calm and assist her recovery. The floor doctor, who thankfully spoke English, interviewed me to make sure I wasn't carrying any infectious diseases.

We were told by the head doctors that Vianna could leave if she wished to, but the standard treatment was 14 days of intravenous antibiotics to be sure that the meningitis had completely gone. They also said something about the airlines not permitting us to travel, but to this day I don't know if this was true or if they just wanted to be sure that the virulent strain of meningitis really had gone before she left the hospital.

I slept on a little fold-down chair each night. I cursed it, but blessed it at the same time, and I would have slept on the floor if necessary. They gave me a blanket, and I felt fortunate that I had been raised on the ranch and was used to roughing it when I had to. Each day I left to catch a cab to my hotel room to shower and clean up. I would wash my clothes in the tub to save time and leave them to dry in the room. Then I would grab some food from the cafeteria when I got back. I learned to sneak food in to Vianna because what they gave her was akin to cardboard. There were times when I flushed the hospital food down the toilet so that they would think that she had eaten it.

Vianna was frazzled and confused during this time, but her recovery was swift after the first week. Each day she was given two courses of intravenous antibiotics from the old glass containers. She had developed phlebitis on both her arms because of the primitive needles they were using. Both arms were yellow, black and blue from fingers to mid-forearm and it became increasingly difficult for the attendants to find a vein.

I was anxious and often frustrated, and, despite the language barrier, could sense the distain and resentment of some of the staff. Remember, this was during the Bush administration and most of the liberal elements in Europe disliked what America was doing. Overall, there were kind people and gruff people there, as in any hospital. I did my best to be polite to everyone, smile as much as I could and put on my best 'wet puppy' demeanor. The cleaning ladies were the worst for me, because each day I

220

had to make myself scarce while they sterilized the room and it was difficult to get back in afterwards because it was still a semi-isolation section and staff who didn't know me would stop me and question me in Italian to find out why I was there. I knew the doctors were bending the rules by letting me be there for Vianna, and I was grateful for it.

The panic attacks that Vianna had were the worst, because all the staff would administer was valerian root in herbal form and this only partly calmed her down. This ordeal was to last two weeks.

Vianna

Throughout this difficult time I still had amazing guidance from above that told me I was going to be okay. I knew that on some spiritual level something significant had happened to me and that I had had to bring myself back in order to move to the next stage as an intuitive healer. Behind it all there was the feeling that I was starting all over again.

Physically, I was like a baby at first. I couldn't stand or go to the bathroom by myself, and eating was difficult. I had come out of the infectious-disease ward incredibly bruised and felt that my whole being had been rebooted.

The first thing I did was to ask Guy for recording equipment. I wanted to record what had happened to me in the coma so that I would never forget it. I also began to touch base with my doctors at home to make sure that they knew what had happened to me and could prepare a treatment plan for when I got home.

When I was in the coma, the nurses had twisted my long hair and put it in a bun. It had stayed like that for some days and had become a knotted mass. Guy began to save what he could of it, spending hours patiently separating it out from the tangles.

Throughout this whole ordeal, Guy did his best to be patient with me and the hospital staff. I think he was afraid that something would happen to me if he left me alone.

Things were improving, though, because we now had an English-speaking doctor who could explain to me what was going on. He was a nice man and treated me with respect.

Finally the 14 days of antibiotics were over. As I was wheeled out of the hospital, I felt as though I was escaping from prison. The crisp winter air of Italy felt good on my face. It was almost Christmas, my favorite time of year, and I was going home…

Guy

Once again Vianna had cheated death and from the darkness of despair had become the phoenix, rising from the ashes to once again breathe the fire of life into her body.

The trip home was harrowing, because we were both paranoid about flying again and the airlines did not come through with their promises of first-class travel. But just before Christmas we made it back to the blessed quiet of our new home.

The Road to Recovery

Vianna

This event changed my life forever. I realized right then that the most important things were my husband, my family, and those who truly loved me. Everything else seemed unimportant. I had come back to life for my children and for Guy. It was the sweet, anguished voices of my husband and daughter that had brought me back. Now I vowed that I would never lose my priorities again. I wouldn't work myself into an early grave. I would grow old with my family beside me.

I started to rebuild myself piece by piece. I was to be under quarantine at home for four weeks because the doctors felt my immune system was compromised, and I could see my children only for short spaces of time. I could eat only very simple foods and was unable to eat proteins of any kind at first. Guy took care of me as one would a little baby.

For a while, all that I did was take care of my physical body. I was unable to make a spiritual connection and so I reached a deeper understanding of those students who were unable to connect daily. I silently apologized to all of them as I finally understood what it was like for them to be in everyone else's reality all the time. I found it overwhelming.

As I got stronger, I began to do my Taoist exercises and to connect and bathe myself in God's Light of the Seventh Plane every day. This was one of the things that put me on the road to recovery and brought me to the realization of what I had been taught about life, death, and divine timing.

Divine Timing

Our divine timing is what we came here to accomplish. It is our accepted mission. That mission might be meeting a person on the street and giving them an insight that changes their life forever. It might be writing a book that changes millions of lives.

It might be working on that little child who goes beyond what we now know of healing and grows back her leg.

I believe that the little coma incident I experienced was somehow part of my divine timing. I think that I brought myself back from the point of death because I wanted to. As far as death is concerned, our divine timing is our own decision. In my case, I think that coming back was something that I set up for myself to see if it was possible. At some level I had to come as close to death as I could and then come back to life – to go to that moment of death and come back. Remember that a month before the coma I had told the class in Rome that I wasn't going to teach DNA 3 until I had raised someone from the dead or come back from a coma. Obviously I was pushing for that experience on some level, to see if it could be done. In ancient times, that was the test: are you good enough to die and come back?

When you are psychic, you have to be careful about interpreting the information that comes to you. For instance, if you go up and see that your divine soul mate will pass away soon after you meet them, it's best not to panic, as this is likely to be just a fear or a belief. I used to be afraid that I'd die on Guy in the early years of our marriage, but I found out that this fear wasn't my own but rather a thought-form from someone else – Guy himself. Truly, it was *his* fear that I would die on him, and nothing to do with a set future event. However, when I met him I knew on some weird level that if I went into a coma, I'd be coming back to life. That's why I told him, 'Don't turn the life-support machine off. I'm coming back.'

When I did come back, I felt very secure and ready to say, 'I have lived this. I know this. I know you can go there and come back. I know you can heal your body. Maybe this isn't something we all ought to experience, but I know it has been part of my divine timing.'

As a child, I had visions of being tied up and locked in a room where no one could hear me. I had a fear of institutions. But these visions and fears were actually about being in Rome in a coma. At that point I was tied up, and I couldn't stand up, because if I had stood up, I'd have blown my heart up because they had given me so much prednisone. And the people around me couldn't hear me – they couldn't understand what I was saying. That was when the flashes from childhood came back: *I've seen this before!*

I've seen a lot of things before. I've seen hectic scenes on Earth. I've seen what will happen if we don't change. I've seen the destruction of the earth – but that can change from day to day. So if you go up and ask, 'Is the earth going to be destroyed?' you're going to get a different answer every day, because we change our beliefs every day.

Many people saw *me* while I was in the coma and they were going about their daily lives and knew nothing of what was happening to me. You see, Guy didn't tell anyone in America except Bobbi and my other children where I was because he wanted to find out if I was going to live or die before he said anything.

When Guy called Bobbi, he told her not to say anything about me being sick. But the very next day my sister Elaine called her, asking where I was and what was wrong with me. Apparently she had seen me standing in her room at night. She said that I had given her something, a form of energy, and told her, 'Hold this for me. I will be back for it.' This made her very worried. She demanded to know what was going on, and Bobbi finally told her.

When I got home from Rome, Elaine called me and told me, 'I have something that belongs to you. You gave it to me while you were in the coma.'

When she gave me back this energy, it seemed that she brought me back to myself and I finally felt whole. It was as if part of me had been lost during the coma and she had given it back to me.

The Aftermath and the New Beginning

The first few months after the coma were very difficult for me. I went to see several doctors for checkups, and from each one I got the same message: what I needed most was time and rest. One of my favorite doctors was very stern with me and told me that I should have limited contact with people for a few months because my immune system was fragile, and I certainly couldn't travel.

You know, he was right: I did need rest and recuperation and I wasn't in any shape to travel. It was strange, but I noticed that I had a difficult time counting and would lose track of where I was, but I could remember everything about diseases and the readings that I had done before.

I have to admit, the congestive heart failure and the coma had scared me, and I wanted to ensure that the information I had gathered over the years was saved for posterity. I began to record many of my experiences and Guy typed them up. This culminated in the *Diseases and Disorders* book that was completed at the end of 2008.

Australian Rainbow Children's Course, February 2008

Guy

The first few months of 2008 were a difficult time for Vianna and me, but even as I watched her struggle for life, we were brought closer together. The reason for this was that more and more we started to live each day as though it was our last together. Some people can't handle hard times – they have sand, not grit. Grit is something that Vianna and I have in abundance – the drive to go forward, even though things don't look so good.

January 2008 was one of these uncharted territories, but Vianna still had the courage to rise from the near-grave and begin a book that was to take a year of my life to compile and complete.

There was, however, a more pressing consideration, and that was how to keep things going. Most people have no concept of what it takes to support several employees with families and run an office, let alone a worldwide modality. Things have to keep moving and bills have to be paid and obligations met. One of these obligations was a Rainbow Children's course that Vianna had been planning for February 2008 in Australia.

Once you have set out to do a seminar and tickets have been bought and deposits collected, considerable investment has been made on both ends of the spectrum, and it's not easy to back out. So, since Vianna couldn't go because of doctor's orders, it was decided that I would go in her stead.

For the two of us to be parted at this tender time was very difficult for both of us. But the bills still had to be paid and we didn't want to disappoint the people who had wanted to be certified in the class. Vianna thought that it would be easier if Josh went with me so that he could help with the class. The Rainbow Children's class is one of the most difficult to coordinate in terms of materials and directing the exercises in the class, and Josh was out of work at the time, so it seemed like a good plan and he agreed to it.

Unfortunately Josh didn't tell his wife, Lindsey, right away, and when he did, she threw a fit and refused to let him go.

When Vianna heard about this, she called up Lindsey to ask her what was going on.

'Josh has to make a living,' she said to her. 'You have to feed your family.'

Lindsey replied, 'He's not leaving me.'

Vianna said, 'Do you mean to tell me that you would rather Josh stay home with you than be able to feed his family?'

Lindsey said, 'Yes!'

Vianna asked her, 'How are you going to get by?'

Lindsey said, 'We will!'

Vianna said, 'Unless one of you gets a job, I'm not going to give you any more money because I am enabling both of you.'

Lindsey began to scream at Vianna and hung up the phone. The two of them didn't speak for months.

So it was that I left for Melbourne to do the class alone.

It was hard to leave Vianna in the house in the middle of winter while I did a class halfway around the world. It would also be the longest we had been apart for nine years.

The trip over was very annoying because the airlines lost my luggage and I arrived with just the clothes I was wearing and none of my office materials. My luggage finally caught up with me two days into the five-day seminar.

I badly missed Vianna and I was very worried about her, especially when a major storm hit Idaho and Vianna was snowed in. Every day I was just looking forward to calling her that night, but my coordinator worked very hard to make the class happen, I had some good help from assistants in the class and, as the Australians say, the class itself was 'full on.'

Being in front of a group of people showed me how challenging it was to be the inspirational speaker for a metaphysical modality, as Vianna had been for so many years. This made me appreciate her even more.

Back to Rome and Back on the Horse

Vianna

When I was a young girl I always wanted to have my own horse. I loved horses. I was fascinated by their beauty, their smell, and their raw power. When I moved to Idaho, I had the opportunity to own a horse and learn how to care for horses. I learned how to feed them, doctor them, and of course how to ride them. I found that they were a big responsibility and also that I was good with them.

One of the things I was taught was that if you were bucked off, you had to get back on that horse right away, or you would never want to ride again. I learned this from a magnificent horse I bought which was what we here in America call 'cut proud.' This means that he still had part of his male genitalia, making him more spirited than usual, and boy, was he spirited! He would go out of his way to get you off his back, and he nearly killed me on several occasions, but I never let him buck me off. On one particular occasion when I was on the ground in front of him, he reared up and acted as though he was going to come down on me with his hooves, but I screamed, 'Stop!' and he backed off and calmed down.

Then I sold this horse and bought an Appaloosa under the mistaken impression that he was a 'kid's horse.' This horse was very difficult and I was bucked off for the first time – and for those of you who have not been bucked off a horse, I can tell you that it is a novel and bone-jarring experience with a certain amount of fear and anger involved that you have to master. But I had been trained that if you got bucked off, you had to get back on, and the sooner, the better. The point I am making is that Rome had become the horse that I had to master and get back on and ride, so I went back there to do a teachers' class and a Rainbow Children's class in the spring of 2008. Guy and I were back on the seminar circuit, determined to ride that horse come what may.

Our previous classes in Rome had always seemed rather strange affairs. Intended for Italians but open to anyone who could speak English or Italian, they had attracted many different nationalities over the years – Spanish, Portuguese, Dutch, British, Irish, Danish... We had had Norwegians, Germans, Austrians, Croats, Slovenes, Israelis, Greeks, Turks, Africans, Australians, New Zealanders, Indians, and Icelanders all together in one room in the sweltering Mediterranean heat. It is a pity we didn't develop the World Relations course earlier – we could all have used it. These classes in Rome were actually influential in the creation of World Relations, because the more we traveled, the more we saw the need to find and deal with hidden negative beliefs relating to other races and cultures.

When I went back to Rome in March 2008, I have to admit I was a little fearful, due to the associations the city now had for me. I was still weak and it was difficult to stand for long periods of time, but somehow I had the strength and energy to teach the class – and to master the fear.

This was a peculiar class because a young Israeli woman became instantly enamored of an Italian man and jumped onto his lap, telling him, 'I don't know why, but I love you.' She began to kiss him passionately. Ah, the romance of Roma! By the look on his face, the young Italian thought that this was a particularly fine set of circumstances, but I had to tell the young woman firmly that she couldn't do that sort of thing in class and had to wait until the break!

The first ThetaHealing Rainbow Children's class in Italy was just as peculiar. What was funny here was that most of the people in the class had never had little children themselves. So when some of the students asked if they could bring their small children to the class, I jumped at the opportunity to show the childless students what teaching children would be like. The little children ran everywhere, making a racket and driving most of the class to distraction. This went on almost nonstop for several days, much to my amusement. Through it all, the energy of the class was dynamic, and we watched many people heal.

After our trip to Italy, Guy and I went back doing classes monthly, but I didn't want to travel as much as in the past but to stay at home more with my family. I decided to start a school in Idaho and have certifications for all of the classes that I taught so that people could take them consecutively. Guy and I found a suitable building in Ammon, Idaho, and began the ThetaHealing Institute of Knowledge. The plan was to do summer classes. We staged the first ones over the summer of 2008, but the most special thing that summer was Bobbi's wedding, and I didn't miss it after all.

Chapter Nineteen

THE VERY ESSENCE OF DUALITY

Any pilot will tell you,
You cannot take off with the wind at your back.
What pushes against you gives you the wind under your wings and
lifts you up.
The challenges of life are like the wind that you face.
Ultimately, they will lift you up so that you can fly.
Delta Airlines

Guy

ThetaHealing was becoming more popular than ever, and it was amazing how many people were showing up with business deals of some kind or other. Offers from internet marketers, network marketers and people who wanted to 'partner out' our business came from many directions. I got to the point where if just one more person had come to Vianna and offered to 'run her business for her,' I would have had something less cordial to say than 'No, thank you.'

Some of these offers were not necessarily bad, just designed to get into the business end of things. Some were more dubious.

We had people offering to set up websites 'for free' that weren't really free. We had people offering to buy our metaphysical store, Nature's Path, and others offering to put the whole thing up for sale online — at a fraction of what it was worth and for a large percentage of the profits. These people fully expected that we would accept their offers. It was things like this that insulted our intelligence.

People forget that Vianna is a psychic as well as a healer. She can see people's intentions and the way that they perceive her. She speaks to her students in simple terms so that everyone can understand her, but I have seen her converse with doctors and geneticists on their own terms. When I asked her about this, she told me, 'It isn't the big words you use that mark you as intelligent. True intelligence is the ability to communicate deep concepts in a simple fashion so that everyone can understand them.'

Few of the offers that were made to us were about healing, but the point is that ThetaHealing is a *healing* modality! *It's about healing.* It wasn't designed as a means of realizing people's grandiose and greedy ambitions.

Several times a year there would be offerings from students to 'join modalities,' i.e., use ThetaHealing as a platform for 'new' modalities, 'the next step in ThetaHealing,' and so on and so forth. The vast majority of these new modalities were in essence variations on the theme of ThetaHealing, and the students proposing them usually knew virtually nothing of the information taught in the advanced classes.

As the modality became more and more popular, people who had caused trouble for Vianna in the past also crawled out from under their rocks to renew their old campaigns and vendettas.

In 2008, we watched all of these energies coalescing in a huge green pool of one human emotion – you know, the one people call *greed*. It was obvious that we had our share of human parasites and a clean-up campaign was in the making.

Vianna still held out hope for the crazy and troublemaking teachers and their appendages, but I suggested we give them their walking papers. By this time we had teachers attacking other teachers, the concept of God, and the concept of free agency, teachers looking for shortcuts in the work and even teachers openly attacking Vianna and me. We had people attempting to sterilize the work and focus only on the scientific, not the spiritual, whereas in ThetaHealing they go hand in hand. We had people removing God so that the only God that people would respect would be *them*. Some of this had been in the works for years before the coma, but after the coma it began to come to a head. By that point, I was more than tired of all the goings-on, and Vianna was stronger and more determined than ever to protect the integrity of the modality. Alas, this was the way that the Creator motivated us to become more organized and to make the modality strong.

I remember the night Vianna sat down with me and manifested that the people with bad intentions for ThetaHealing leave in the most beneficial way. Looking back, I can see that she got her wish.

By the end of the summer, Joshua was having money problems and was breaking up with Lindsey. When he left her for another woman, it was a case of hell hath no fury like a woman scorned. Vianna still helped Lindsey and her father during this time with money and found them a place to live in Idaho Falls. She was concerned about her grandchildren. One day, however, Lindsey told Vianna she had to choose between her and Joshua. She said she would keep the grandchildren from Vianna if she had further contact with Josh. Vianna wasn't prepared to lose contact with her son. She told Lindsey, 'No grandchildren, no more money.' Lindsey stormed out. The lines in the dirt had been drawn.

Vianna believes that her children are free to live their own lives. Their personal experiences and relationships are their own and she doesn't interfere in matters of the heart. But she does expect her children and their spouses to show respect and pay their own bills.

Lindsey left the state, and a bitter divorce and long-term custody battle ensued. At the end of 2008, Joshua decided to resign as a teacher of ThetaHealing because of all the controversy.

At the beginning of 2009 the teachers who had been causing us problems were asked to leave the modality. We felt that since they didn't want to teach the work as it was given, they should have the opportunity of teaching what they wanted, but without using ThetaHealing as a platform. When people come to learn ThetaHealing, it is a misrepresentation to teach something completely different and still call it ThetaHealing.

Opinions were expressed, sometimes forcefully, but they say that there is no such thing as bad publicity, and they are right. Our book sales doubled almost immediately.

When someone actually claimed that the Creator was an evil entity, Vianna was very hurt and felt the need to fight for God, but then the Creator told her, 'The energy of All That Is doesn't need to be defended. It just is. Step away from this, Vianna, and watch the All That Is do its magic.'

Suddenly we were approached by many spiritual and religious organizations, all asking us to come and teach. The Sivananda Yoga ashram in the Bahamas, one of the largest yoga organizations in the world, was one of them, and we decided to be married while we were doing classes there. Just as on the occasion of our first marriage 12 years before, Vianna was late because she was having her hair done, in this case by the Japanese students who had come to take the class. This marriage was a rather elaborate affair with a genuine tantric priest marrying us Hindu style. We received blessings from the head swamis, and the ceremony was a very spiritual ritual that we enjoyed very much.

This gave us stronger motivation to state that ThetaHealing was a God modality and we believed in free agency. It also gave us the motivation to register our trademark.

What was surprising to me was that Vianna's manifestation prayer had removed the troublemaking people in her life in such a way as to permit ThetaHealing to grow exponentially.

There are no accidents in this world, and Vianna and I both believe we have learned a great deal about the depravity to which the human condition can stoop and the soaring heights to which it can ascend. We have learned a lot about standing strong and not dropping to someone else's level. Eventually we ignored the conflict and went on with our lives.

After 14 years of living with Vianna, I have found the most wonderful thing about her is her boundless faith in people. This is not to say that she doesn't see their unpredictability, nor is she blind to the possibility that they may attempt to take advantage of her, but when she looks at a person, she chooses to see their potential for goodness and gives them a chance. This quality can be perceived as weakness, but we shouldn't confuse kindness with weakness. Vianna realizes that we all have light and darkness within us. Her real role in this life is to give people the opportunity to go to the light.

Vianna

When Guy and I started to write this book, it made us examine our lives from the standpoint of the past to the present. So much has happened in the past 14 years, and many of these experiences hadn't been properly processed. We found out that it was necessary to work on our beliefs about the unprocessed past. Upon reflecting on it, it seemed to us that it was through conflict that we grew as people. This may have had something to do with the beliefs of other people and little to do with us; however, we did need to learn how to grow without unnecessary conflict. This was an important lesson for us both.

Chapter Twenty
NEW HOPE

The Teachers' Seminar, Japan, March 2009

Guy

The second time we went to Japan to certify teachers, things went much more smoothly than the first. With the help of other key people, Hiroyuki Miyazaki had made ThetaHealing much more streamlined for the practitioners and teachers than it had been before.

The second certification class was held in Tokyo, with 80 students attending. Tokyo was a fascinating city. Hiro told us that 31 million people lived there, not to mention those who commuted there every day. The metropolis was almost overwhelming when seen from a tall building, because it extended for 1,359 square miles – as far as the eye could see in every direction. It had the appearance of being very orderly and clean. The streets looked scrubbed and there was no trash.

This class proved to us that interest in ThetaHealing was growing in Japan. But for us, the special thing about this visit was the Enkakuji monastery and Vianna's experience there.

Hiro had arranged for us to go to a Buddhist temple and monastery called Enkakuji, by Kamakura city in the Kanagawa prefecture. This Zen Buddhist monastery had been founded in the 1200s and it was said that some of the remains of the Buddha were stored in a grotto in the middle of the temple grounds.

We rode on one of the passenger trains that are so prevalent in Japan, arriving at the monastery complex at midday. The hustle and bustle of Tokyo was behind us and the temple grounds were a perfect Japanese garden. The blossom was just beginning to come out on the trees and the spirits of the place could be perceived on the winds that teased the leaves. It took little to imagine yourself transported back in time.

The presiding Buddhist monk, who asked for Vianna to give him a healing, gave us a tour of the grounds and grotto. We were allowed to see the altar that is only open to the public once a year – they opened it up specially for us.

Vianna

When I stepped up to the grotto, I felt a sharp pain in my chest. It was as if an electric shock had passed through my body. It was gone in the same instant. Then I began to feel a strange tingling throughout my body, followed by the sensation of having rose petals rain down on me while hearing the essence of laughter. I asked the universe, 'What is this?' and heard, 'This is compassion.'

I was confused by this answer because I thought I knew what compassion felt like. I had downloaded it into myself and it hadn't felt like this.

I was answered with the message: 'This is what the compassion of the Buddha feels like. Everyone who has developed true compassion has a feeling that is their own, and this is the compassion of the Buddha.'

After our visit to the grotto, we walked back to the little shop where they were selling spiritual gifts for the benefit of the monastery. I walked up to the small buddha section, picked out a buddha that I was drawn to and took it up to buy it. I expected it to be a buddha of protection, because at the time I was being attacked on the internet. But when I asked what kind it was I was told that it was a buddha of mercy. This message disappointed me because it was telling me that I should have mercy towards those who had been taken in by the deceptions of others. Somehow I had to find a way to forgive them. I took the buddha home and followed the message.

Tsuyoshi Kushida, Japanese Neurosurgeon

In 2008, a Japanese neurosurgeon, Tsuyoshi Kushida, known by his nickname of Hub-K, became interested in ThetaHealing. He told us that doctors in Japan were more open to energy healing than those in the West since there was not such a stigma attached to it. Using the Theta brainwave as a platform, an effort is being made in Japan to bridge the gap between the energy-healing world and conventional medicine.

In 2009 Hub-K began to develop a website to gather raw data from healings and assess their validity from a conventional medical standpoint. He introduced the work to the creator of the artificial heart, who allowed him to research ThetaHealing in his clinic. Hub-K also formed the ThetaHealing® Medical Association of Japan & Asia and the Staff of ISLIS (International

Society of Life Information Science). In 2010 he wrote a book entitled *How to Become Healthy Using the Theta Brainwave*. Vianna was thrilled with his vision.

While we were in Japan, Hub-K had rented a restaurant and invited the class to a party. Dr. Kazuhiko Atsumi, pioneer of artificial heart research, came so that he could meet with Vianna. He told her that he had explored all the different kinds of medicine and now it was time to explore spiritual healing. He was a delightful man and during the party danced with his wife like a man 20 years younger than he was. Many of the students took their turn in the fine art of karaoke, and we found that Hub-K was very talented at singing karaoke.

Jenaleighia and the RV Wreck

Vianna

One of my best teachers in faith has been my granddaughter Jenaleighia, the first baby to have the DNA activation before she was born. As she grew older, she began to project her simple enlightenment as only a Rainbow Child can. Her great insight has often inspired me and filled me with awe, as has her understanding.

In 2009 Guy and I decided to purchase two recreation vehicles so that we could explore the mountains. We wanted to take the family up there and just have fun. I was against Jena or any of the children riding the RVs, but Jena pestered Guy sweetly until he let her drive one, unbeknownst to me. He thought I was just being overprotective and didn't know that I had an uneasy feeling about it.

Sure enough, one day Jena was riding the Yamaha Rhino with Bobbi's stepsister Liz driving. They were in an open field, so Bobbi wasn't worried about them. But when Liz turned to go down a side road, she tipped over the Rhino on Jena's side and Jena was seriously injured. She had put her arm out to brace herself and it had been crushed by the roll bar while she was trapped in the Rhino by the seatbelt.

Luckily some people who were camping nearby saw the wreck and came to help her out. It was Jena's good fortune that one of these people was a nurse, another was a dispatcher, and the third was from the military medical division. When Bobbi got there ten minutes later, these wonderful people already had Jena bandaged up and secure.

Jena kept repeating, 'Please call my grandma. Just call my grandma and I will be okay, and in only ten minutes I can go play.' Even in the ambulance she was telling the paramedics, 'If you call my grandma I will be okay.' But when they arrived at the hospital, the pulse in her hand was so faint it wasn't even reading on the equipment.

I was already waiting at the hospital. Jena looked up at me and said, 'Grandma, will you work on me?'

'Of course I will, sweetheart,' I told her, doing my best to be composed.

As I worked on Jena's arm, the surgical specialist was talking to Bobbi in the hall so that Jena couldn't hear. He told her, 'From what the ER doctors tell me, they may have to amputate your daughter's arm. She has crushed the nerves and punctured the main artery. She is lucky to have made it this far. She could have easily died from the trauma.'

Bobbi started to cry and Jena heard her. She said to me, 'Will you go outside and take care of my mom?'

I went out to the hall and talked to Bobbi. Then she went into the room and told Jena she was all right.

Next the doctor went into Jena's room. He listened to her arm and found that there was now a faint pulse. He took Bobbi back out into the hall and told her, 'Okay, they will be able to operate, but I can't make any guarantees that she will ever get back the use of her hand or fingers.'

Jena went into surgery. After six and a half hours, the doctor came into the waiting room and said, 'Her arm was like a hamburger and it took a lot to repair it. We had to take a section of a vein from her leg to reconnect the artery in her arm. Everything looks good and we will know more tomorrow. There may be a large amount of swelling due to the arm being so long without blood flow, so they may have to make some incisions in her forearm. Now that I am done, the bone doctor is going to set her bone, and he will come and speak to you soon.'

Thirty minutes later the second doctor came in and told us, 'The bone looks great! It was an easy setting. We washed and cleaned the bone, but we had to put pins in the arm because of the wound from the fracture. She will have to wear the fixture for about 10 to 12 weeks. I will check on her tomorrow. Thank you.'

Greatly relieved, we all thanked the doctor. Jena's arm was saved because of the brilliant healing hands of the surgeons.

The next morning, both doctors were surprised that Jena's pulse was strong and there was no swelling in the arm.

The doctors told Bobbi that so much skin had been lost that in six to eight weeks they would consider performing a skin graft to cover the wound, but Jena said calmly, 'No, thank you. I will be better in no time. I will just have my grandma work on it.'

After three days on IV antibiotics, Jena went home. After nine weeks, the open wound had completely healed and no skin graft was necessary. The doctors didn't say much about this except, 'It looks great!' The nurses, however, told Jena they had never seen anything like that heal so quickly.

Jena had the pins removed in the doctor's office with no anesthesia. She is one brave little girl. She has now regained full movement in her fingers and can shoot the gun on her video game. If you ask her why she healed so fast she will tell you it was because of ThetaHealing.

The United Kingdom, 2009

In 2009 we went to London to do our first teachers' certification class there. We hadn't been to the UK for some time, though one of our early teachers had taught some classes there, which had generated interest in ThetaHealing.

Our coordinator, Christen, had arranged for us to go to the Isle of Skye in Scotland. This was an unexpected and very nice thing for her to do for us. The trip was magical and we enjoyed it very much. Our bus driver was a modern-day druid and had a good grasp of the history of Scotland.

When we reached Skye, the land triggered a memory that answered a question that had been in my mind for some years. When I first met Guy I used to say, 'I'm sorry, I can't have your son.' I kept saying this, even though I didn't want any more children and Guy wasn't asking me to have any more either. It was very strange.

Then Guy gave me a Celtic music tape called *Celtic Women of Song*. I seemed to know one of the songs and could sing all the words, even though they were in Gaelic. Then I had a flashback of myself as a woman with long red hair, rocking a baby as I waited for my husband to come home. It seems that he was the first mate on a shipping boat and I loved him dearly. I could see myself singing this song and pining for him to come home to me.

In order to find out what was going on, I had a friend take me down into a crystal layout. She took me back to being the woman with long red hair. I remembered talking to my husband, whom I presume was Guy. I loved him and told him that I would give him five boys, but I died of a hemorrhage while giving birth to our fourth son. The last words that I said to my love were, 'I'm so sorry that I didn't have your fifth son.'

This memory was very powerful, and I speculated on where the events had taken place. First I thought that it had to be Ireland, because it had lots of ports. But when Guy and I went to Ireland, the land didn't have the energy that I had felt in the vision. When we went to the Isle of Skye, however, I realized that this was the place where we had been so in love. It was amazing to relive that feeling once again in all its majesty.

Guy

The bus ride was a whirlwind of sights and sensations, both on the drive north and on the drive back to Edinburgh. When we got back to Edinburgh, we decided to treat ourselves to a short trip to Rosslyn Chapel. I found this enchanting, in spite of the renovation work that was being carried out on it. This church is the foundation for many people's belief systems, from masons to Christian conspiracy theorists.

We flew back to England to do a talk at St James's Church in London. Vianna made a speech to a sold-out house and I was never more proud of her than I was that night. She seemed to emanate light, and I will always remember how she was on fire with her oration.

During the teachers' class, we met a woman named Susie Pearl, who was definitely an embodiment of an angel of compassion. The energy that emanated from her when she talked about ThetaHealing was a wholesome essence that reminded one of freshly baked bread.

Susie decided that the world should know about ThetaHealing, so she called a friend of hers at Hay House Publishing named Michelle.

Vianna

After Michelle had reviewed our books, she signed us up to a book deal the very next day. As if by magic in one of the most amazing twists of fate, we were launched with a major publishing company with a reputation for being fair and honest.

This was such a relief for me. I was tired of the challenge of self-publishing, printing, and translating the books.

We left Britain full of new hope.

Chapter Twenty-One

TRAVELING THROUGH THE EARTH CHANGES

Guy

Just a few months into 2010, Mother Nature began to deliver deadly natural disasters at a rate that was higher than normal – and Vianna and I were traveling through them.

In January we were on the Gold Coast, Australia, when a devastating earthquake hit Haiti, killing 230,000 people. The high number of causalities led some to call this earthquake the worst natural disaster to occur in modern times.

Then on February 27, an earthquake with a magnitude of 8.8 was recorded off the central Chilean coast. This triggered a tsunami which devastated several coastal towns. Tsunami warnings were issued in 53 countries and over 500 people lost their lives.

This earthquake happened when we were on vacation in Maui. We hadn't been on a vacation in years, it had been ten years since we had been to Maui, and we wanted to go back to Hana Bay House, the romantic house that we had rented the first time we had been to the Hawaiian Islands. This time Vianna wanted to take all of her children along so that she could share the experience with them.

We had the usual harrowing drive to Hana, up the endless winding road with deep chasms and mega vegetation. We dropped the children off at their own rental house in Hana so that they could be alone (and we could as well), and continued up the coast to our romantic destination.

When we walked in the door of the Hana Bay House, we found that while some of the furniture had changed, the rest of the house had stayed the same. It was if it had been frozen in time, waiting for us to return. What struck us was that *we* had changed – exponentially. After ten years of traveling around the world, teaching thousands of people ThetaHealing, writing four books (and the attached 16 manuals), and experiencing the joy and heartache that can be associated with the birth of a healing modality, we had grown as people, particularly in the last three years. It was nice to see that the past was still there, and the memories of dancing to the music from *Message in a Bottle*, Vianna eating her first papaya and dreaming of the goddess Pele were all treasures, but it was the future that was the most important.

It was in the early hours of the fourth day that we were awakened by a frantic phone call from Joshua telling us about the tsunami that had hit Chile. There was a danger that it was also going to hit Hawaii. Then we heard the warning sirens going off in the town of Hana.

The last time that a tsunami had been created by an earthquake in Chile, it had devastated Maui, so a wave of hysteria rippled across the island. The kids were ordered to evacuate their low-lying apartment for the sake of safety, and we headed up the road to Hana, seeking higher ground. It wasn't that we were afraid of the tsunami, as Vianna felt that things would be okay, but we did want to be able to get out of the rather remote Hana so that we could catch our plane home. There was also the added concern of hysteria on the part of other people. So we took the road from Hana to Kahului and went to a campsite in the mountains to wait until the tsunami had hit and the hysteria was over. We made a fire, ate the food from the cooler that Brennan, Bobbi's husband, had brought, and had a good time at the campsite.

When the tsunami danger was over, there was no fuel to be had because everyone had stocked up. We had barely enough gas to get down the road to Hana. Throwing our fate to the winds, we canceled our stay at the Hana Bay House and headed down to one of the towns outside Kahului in the hopes of getting fuel. We pulled into a small tourist town at the base of the road that led to Hana, and just barely got fueled up before the fuel pump shut down due to lack of petrol.

Still uncertain where we were going to stay or if there were any hotel rooms available, we decided to head into Kahului. All the cell-phone networks had been shut off, and it wasn't until we reached the outskirts of the town that we got our phones working again. When we called the resorts to see if there were any rooms, we were told that there were none to be had. All the kids were tired and carsick from the drive, so we went to McDonald's in the hope of getting an internet connection. Bobbi did such fancy footwork on the computer that like magic we had rooms booked at a Marriott at the other end of the island.

The remaining two days of the trip were idyllic, as we all relaxed from the harrowing experience. We made some deals shopping, enjoyed the rainbows in the sky, and even made our flight on time.

I guess we learned that you can go back in time and Hana will remain the same; it is you who will have changed.

We had one more adventure with the Earth changes that year that showed us how she could shake the ground and darken the skies.

Eyjafjallajökul Volcano

In April 2010 we were in Italy when the Eyjafjallajökul volcano erupted in Iceland, causing enormous disruption to air travel across western and northern Europe over an initial period of six days. Then, beginning on April 14, the eruption entered a second phase and created an ash cloud that led to the closure of most of Europe's airspace for another five days.

During all this we flew into the UK to do a class there, wondering if we were going to make it home anytime soon, since all flights to America were canceled. I was a little nervous about getting home, but Vianna told me it would be fine, and in spite of the backlog of flights, we did make it home on time.

~~~~~

It seemed that every time we traveled in 2010, the Earth burped, so I was relieved to start the summer classes at home. I knew that the energy was shifting and the classes had very good people in them.

When we finished our classes at home, we were excited by the prospect of going to Mexico City for the first time. I knew it would be a life-changing event.

Chapter Twenty-Two

LIFE-CHANGING SEMINARS

Teachers' Class, Mexico City, Mexico, 2010

Renata Braun was the first teacher to be certified from Mexico and was the only one from the early years to stay the distance with ThetaHealing Mexico and see the *ThetaHealing* book translated into Spanish. She had the patience of a saint over this. The translation had languished for a very long time with a lady from Florida, and when we finally got it back from her, it needed further editing. Renata and Antonio, another teacher, did this out of the goodness of their hearts and the need to have the book for their students. They both took all the classes, and Antonio decided to leave a successful drafting job to start ThetaHealing Mexico with Renata.

Vianna and I flew into Mexico City on an October day, punching through the clouds of smog and landing in another world – a world that is just across the border from the United States.

We didn't know what to expect. For a few years there had been unrest along the border states of Mexico and the United States due to drug trafficking. We were reasonably certain that this did not affect Mexico City, but I am a cautious man as it relates to my wife. Many of our friends and families were concerned about our going there, but we went because of our hosts Renata and Antonio, and others there that love the work. This is our life. This is what we do.

Admittedly it gave us pause when Renata and Antonio picked us up in a bulletproof SUV borrowed from one of their more affluent students. Two questions immediately arose: 1. Why do we need a bulletproof car? And 2. Why do we need a bulletproof car?

Antonio and Renata brushed off our queries in true Spanish style. We felt that the die had been cast, so we settled into our fate.

We drove through Mexico City, entranced by the endless sprawl and the dichotomy of magnificent buildings and dire poverty. It struck me that Mexico is still an Aztec nation in spite of all that has happened to the people since the Spanish conquistadors came in the 1500s. Many of the faces that I saw were Native American or Indian mix, with Indian dominant in most. When I looked into the eyes of some of these people, I felt transported back to a time when the fierce Indian tribes still ruled the city of the eagle and the rattlesnake.

As we drove through the pea-soup smog to our hotel, we were informed by Antonio and Renata that we would be going on a hike the next day up a popular trail leading to some temples. We dutifully nodded our heads in agreement.

Armed guards patrolled the hotel, but this didn't bother us, since we were used to firearms. If there was a need for such things, then such things were needed.

The hotel doubled as a hot disco and party place for young people, as we were to find out that weekend. Mexico City is party central, and the taste of wildness is in the air as you walk the streets.

After we had freshened up, Antonio and Renata fed us our first real Mexican food, which we enjoyed very much. We went to bed exhausted and full of culture shock.

When Antonio and Renata came to pick us up in the morning we avoided Montezuma's revenge by a shot of thyme to kill the bacteria that we weren't used to and went on the adventure into the clouds that we had been promised.

On the drive there along the modern highway, I saw grain being harvested in the old way. Shocks of grain were tied into bundles in the fields and apparently most of the grain was still put up by hand.

We came to the little town of Tepoztlán at the base of the mountain we were about to climb and began walking up the trail to the clouds. At the base of the trail there was a market on both sides of the street. This was fascinating to us: the wares that were set out for sale were as varied as any I had ever seen. We sampled some cooked and peppered grasshoppers and I found them quite tasty, if a bit crunchy. Market stalls were also set up along the trail leading to the temples several thousand feet higher. They finally petered out when the trail became steeper and turned into stairs that led endlessly upward to the temple of Tepozteco.

What some people might not realize about Mexico is that the altitude is very high, even on the valley floor, so we were a little out of breath before we even started the climb. It took several hours of arduous climbing to get to the 8,858 foot peak where the temples were. A sharp salesman was selling water at the small and anti-climactic temple complex and enjoying brisk business.

What was surprising to us was the number of people who came to climb the winding stairs into the clouds. We must have passed hundreds coming and going along the trail.

When we had purchased some water, it was time to get down the mountain before the light faded; indeed, it was dark when we finally got to the bottom, where we passed two soldiers going up the trail with rifles. Antonio told us that this was to protect the people still walking the trail from bandits.

Hungry from our exertions, we had dinner in one of the restaurants of the village and had a great meal. Antonio and Renata happily told us that we were going to the huge temple complex of Teotihuacan the next day. We did our best not to appear too alarmed, thinking that perhaps this time we would be scaling a Mexican Mount Everest! Antonio and Renata laughingly assured us that we wouldn't have to climb any more mountains. That night, we fell into our hotel bed exhausted but happy.

We woke the next day with sore muscles but game for the next adventure. Our happy and glowing hosts told us that we were going to the Temples of the Sun and the Moon and also meeting a Mexican dignitary whose daughter was a ThetaHealer.

The dignitary met us at the temples, surrounded by his retinue, and gave us a tour of a tunnel complex that had been dug underneath the Temple of the Sun by the original builders. We climbed down ladders with the dignitary's bodyguards around us, down into the bowels of the temple to see a machine that was somehow mapping the temple using sonic waves.

Then we were invited to have breakfast in the dignitary's vast hacienda. A plumed priest and priestess in beautiful feathered costumes awaited us there and welcomed and blessed us with a copal smudging and an ancient song. We were then ushered into a spacious hall to be seated at the head of the table next to the dignitary and his wife. Helpers offered us dishes that were very different from anything we had seen before. The dignitary told us that we were dining as the ancient Aztec kings had, complete with cooked mealworms and ant eggs with herbs! We sampled both dishes and found them to be delicious, in spite of the way they looked.

When we finished the meal, we were driven back to the temple complex and taken to a new excavation, where Vianna and the dignitary had a discussion about the temple. I took some pictures of the hieroglyphs on the floors of the place, and then we left to tour the rest of the complex. The dignitary left, and we were given an armed guard to watch over us for the rest of the day as we walked around incredible pyramids that rivaled any ancient ruins the world over for majesty and architectural magnificence.

The next day was the Day of the Dead festival, an old holiday dating back to the Aztec Empire. It was once centered on the Aztec god of death, Mictlantecuhtli, and the thousands of Mexicans who came into the city to celebrate all seemed to be brandishing some kind of skeleton or skull. A correlation of this festival is our own holiday, Halloween, which was originally a festival of the dead in pre-Christian times.

The next day we started the classes and were greeted by some of the most wonderful people to have as teachers. The class was amazing! Two of them, both tiny ladies, had even come from one of the outlying Indian villages and couldn't read, but learned by listening to Renata's translation of Vianna's teachings. Once we had finished the first day of class, we had fallen in love with Old Mexico.

One night after class, Antonio and Renata took us to the spiritual bazaar in the middle of town. This was one of the most interesting things of all, as we found it to be a warren of spiritual articles for sale, both Christian and pagan, as well as a fusion of the two. Angels and demons rubbed shoulders with ancient Aztec gods, not to mention voodoo, *bruja*, and *curandera* articles. Articles for curses, prayers, and fertility were ranged haphazardly on the same shelves. Rows and rows of herbs of every description went on endlessly in every direction, piled as high as the ceiling. In some places it was difficult to walk down the alleyways and not bump into some of the wares.

The students at the classes were very enthusiastic throughout our stay there. Throughout the classes Antonio played *The Fountain* by Clint Mansell, the heartrending soundtrack to the movie of the same name.

What Mexico reminded Vianna and me was that life is all about love, and that is what we felt from Old Mexico on this first trip. When the class was over, we left with a warm, happy feeling, knowing that ThetaHealing was going strong in Mexico and everyone was working wonderfully well together.

Teachers' Class, New Delhi, India

Very few western teachers of spiritual modalities are awarded the opportunity of teaching in India. Most people go to India to *learn* from India. We learned from it, too, but the special thing that we found there was the ease with which ThetaHealing was accepted by the Indians. It was as easy as breathing to them.

We were greeted in India with flowers that were thrown at Vianna's feet from the airport all the way out to the cars. This was a little overwhelming, but we were honored by it.

Sumant Kaul, a teacher, and later our coordinator for India, had taken the work into himself with a passion that I cannot describe. He was one of the most amazing men we had ever met.

The first thing that strikes you about New Delhi is the contrast between rich and poor. It is a different world, a place so culturally distinct from all that you are used to as to be surreal. Like the Mexicans, the people weren't burdened by the materialism that oppresses some of the western world, and the students were loving and passionate about the work.

As we drove up to the hotel, we were struck by the everyday challenges that are faced by Indians. As was customary, our car was searched for bombs before we were admitted to the hotel, and there was also a security check at the door for weapons and bombs.

The Hotel Radisson was a beautiful place with fine architecture. As we looked out of the window, we saw that it shared its grounds with the fierce-looking monkeys who lived wild right in the middle of New Delhi.

The Indian people seem to have a spiritual intensity about them. Whether Hindu or Muslim, they are very serious about what they believe. We were delighted when we found that our class also had some Sikhs attending, with their beautiful turbans.

There were over 100 people in the class, and these wonderful people truly embraced us. Vianna was even given a World Peace Award at a banquet in her honor for the creation of a healing modality designed to create peace.

The intent of the ThetaHealing World Relations Class is to release national and cultural prejudices that slow our spiritual development.

We fell in love with Sumant's family, and after class his tall and handsome son gave us a demonstration of Bollywood dancing that delighted the ladies.

As we watched Indian television at night, it seemed to us that there was some kind of continuous scandal going on, going round and round like a revolving door. The other thing that stood out about Indian television was the Bollywood presentations. We fell in love with the music and acting, even though we couldn't understand much of what was said. There seems to be a strong reclamation of national culture going on in the world's largest democracy, which has over a billion people and a huge economy that will soon rival that of China.

When the class was over, Sumant had arranged for us to go to Jaipur, in the state of Rajasthan, to look at some of the gem and jewelry production there. We left in two cars early in the morning and got our first taste of travel in India. Even the traffic in Rome pales into insignificance in comparison. It is a wonder to me how there isn't a wreck of some kind every ten minutes or so. Most of the traffic on the road we took to Jaipur consisted of lumbering transport trucks whose drivers seemed to proceed willy-nilly with no thought that there was anyone else in the world, let alone on the road.

As we drove along, Sumant told us that India operated by prayer, and that statement was graphically demonstrated to us by the way that drivers narrowly missed hitting a 2,000-pound Brahma bull that placidly walked out in front of them, by the elephant riding in the back of an open truck without restraints of any kind, by the huge backhoe that was only restrained with a small rope and by the truck carrying a huge cotton cargo that was hanging out on all sides and taking up most of the road. The honking of horns never stopped the whole way to Jaipur, and when I went to bed that night I could still hear them in my dreams.

The next morning we saw the enthralling process of jewelry creation, from the basic casting of the metal findings to the cutting and faceting of the raw stones into glittering gems. This was fascinating to me as a metalsmith, and I wanted to stay and learn each step of every process.

We saw various jewelry hotspots; at one place, I was shown a blue sapphire as big as a hen's egg, and at another shop, gaudy costume jewelry. All the street people were hoping to make an easy profit from the westerners, but we had our ace in the hole – actually, two of them. The first was Sumant, who could bargain with a bulldozer, and the second was a friend of his who knew the area. These two made sure that our purchases were fairly priced.

Outside one of the shops a tiny beggar girl came up to Vianna and asked for money. Vianna gave her some and noticed that she had jaundice. Her skin was yellow, as were her eyes. Vianna asked her if she could do a healing on her. The little girl took her money and her healing and happily scampered behind us for a while before disappearing off into the streets of Jaipur. Vianna cried when she left, and we will never know what happened to her.

The next day we started back to New Delhi on a trip that was supposed to take four hours. Unfortunately, it took ten, because of the traffic. We had to pack rather hurriedly so that we could make our plane. We said goodbye to our hosts and flew home, happy with our amazing trip to India.

Teachers' Class, Japan 2011

Courage is not the absence of fear... but rather the judgment that something else is more important than fear.
You may not live forever, but the over-cautious do not live at all.

Guy Stibal

The day before the devastating tsunami hit Japan, Vianna had Bobbi send an e-mail to Hiro Miyazaki inquiring if he was safe from the earthquake that she felt had hit Japan. He wrote back the same day and told her that there was no earthquake. But the next day he knew what she was talking about.

On March 11, 2011, the massive 9.0-magnitude earthquake that struck near the northeastern coast of Japan created a tsunami that hit just minutes afterwards. We had scheduled a teachers' certification on April 7, and from the early reports of the devastation I wondered if the airlines would be flying to Japan. Then, when the ongoing tragedy at the Fukushima nuclear power plant brought fears of radiation sweeping through the world at large, many people started leaving Japan because of concerns over the release of radiation from the dysfunctional reactors.

What surprised me was Vianna's response right from the beginning of the disaster. First, she wept for the people who had died in the tsunami. Then, as the reports turned from bad to worse, I asked her if we would have a class in Japan and she responded clearly, 'Of course we're going. Everything will be fine. Now is the time that our students need us the most.'

In the weeks before the class, Vianna never wavered in her conviction about going to Japan, even when military families left the country and some of her Japanese students called her, telling her that she should stay home because of the radiation concerns and hysteria over shortages of food, water, and electricity (which proved to be largely unfounded). Vianna told me that if her Japanese students were still intent on coming, she was still intent on teaching them. She knew that some of the students who were coming to the class had lost their homes, and this made her even more determined. We both felt that the Japanese had always been good to us and we wouldn't abandon them at this dark time.

Our friends and family were incredulous when we told them that we were still going to Japan. Even at the airport, when I gave in my luggage to be scanned at security, one of the TSA agents looked at me and said, 'Feel the need for radiation?'

To which I replied, 'I guess so.'

The trip started with a rumble. As we arrived and gave our passport to a controller, a 7.0 earthquake shook the building. Tokyo was more subdued than we had experienced before, but still operating with a 'business as usual' attitude. The hotel, however, was like something out of a ghost town, almost devoid of people except for the staff.

There were admittedly some problems up north with the nuclear plant, but we knew the authorities were doing their best to manage the situation. The people most at risk were the brave workers who had contained the problem and the people who were still living close to the plant.

The aftershocks were mainly tiny, but there were some rather large ones that were a little disconcerting. One, which occurred in the evening, while we were at our hotel, was a 7.1 magnitude quake. Another of these larger aftershocks, a 7.6 magnitude quake, came at the end of the Basic Teachers' class and the Japanese students carried on, unconcerned about the shaking building. Alarms went off that no one listened to and the people who were writing names on the chalkboard for the last healing continued to do so undeterred. We were actually taking a picture during the earthquake and everyone politely pretended not to notice that the room was shaking.

We were teaching on the 40th floor of the Mora Building, so when the elevators shut down for a safety check, the whole class was essentially stranded. Everyone was calm and collected until the elevators began working again, and then 211 students and 30 support teachers happily left the building with their new certifications in ThetaHealing.

Five or more aftershocks hit daily, making us a little on edge. The Japanese were experiencing a kind of seasickness from the Earth moving so much. This didn't surprise me at all, having experienced just a fraction of the trauma that the Japanese had gone through since the beginning of the crisis.

We were interviewed by *Natural Spirit* magazine, a metaphysical publication in Japan, four days into one of our classes. The first question was: 'Why are you here? Everyone else who was staging spiritual events in Japan has cancelled. Why did you come?'

Vianna replied, 'Now is the time that Japan needs healing. If my students want me to come, then I will come.'

The interviewers asked, 'Are you concerned about the radiation?'

Vianna told them, 'No, the levels in Tokyo aren't dangerous, but I have the advantage of knowing a fair amount about radiation from my training in nuclear security. Besides, God told me that it would be fine to come and teach, so I did.'

There was no answer to that one.

Chapter Twenty-Three

FORTY DAYS AND FORTY NIGHTS... IN EUROPE

At the beginning of May 2011, Vianna and I went on a whirlwind tour of Europe. It is trips like these that can make a person think that their schedule is a bit full...

The trip started in Italy with a teachers' seminar in Rome. Then it was onward to a soul-mate class and the Mind, Body, Spirit festival in London. After that it was on to Germany to do basic and advanced introductory classes with our new coordinators there, then back to London for events connected with the release of the *Advanced ThetaHealing* book.

We were gone 40 days. That is a long time to be away from home. I know that many people romanticize travel. They think of adventure, new faces and places, exotic dining, shopping and romantic candlelight dinners. The reality can be very different...

This is not to say that Vianna and I haven't benefited from travel. It has expanded our minds as nothing else could have done. We now see the world as interconnected and becoming more so every day. But the fact remains that when you travel to teach classes as we do, the hours are long and the work doesn't stop when the class is over. There is always someone who needs a healing after class from Vianna, and people call her at all hours of the night, owing to the time difference in other countries. Calls in the middle of the night are common even after a 16-hour day of registration, coordination, class teaching, paperwork, book signings, and healings, then driving to the hotel and being too tired to go out for dinner, so that all is left is room service (if you are lucky enough to have room service) and bed... with the night too short and a mind that sometimes refuses to shut down after the events of the day, to say nothing of the effects of jet-lag. If your mind won't shut down, this also means that your thoughts are loud and can bother your psychic wife when she is trying to sleep. When you live with a psychic, there is also the influx of intuitive impressions that come to them, unbidden and without warning – everything from psychic messages from students and premonitions about the next day to ghosts coming to call. All these things are sleep disturbances, and sleep on the road is a precious commodity. Getting this precious sleep can also be difficult depending on the hotel you are staying at, the type of bed you are sleeping in and the general environment you find yourself in. Each place you stay at will have its own particular energy.

Rome, Italy

When we started off our tour in Rome, we experienced the wonderful passion that is so typical of the Italians. The class was a bit difficult in the way of coordination, however, so both Vianna and I were a little tired by the time it was over.

London, England

We flew out to our next appointment, a four-hour introductory class at the Mind, Body, Spirit festival in London and a new soul-mate certification class at the Columbia Hotel. When we landed, we found that our luggage hadn't made it onto the same flight as us.

When we got to our four-star central London hotel (not the Columbia), we were tired and a little strung out from the road. The hotel was old, as are many of the buildings in London, but the rooms were nice and clean.

Vianna couldn't sleep that first night and, true to form, something strange happened. I was peacefully sleeping when she grabbed my arm and shook me awake. With a great sense of urgency in her voice, she said, 'Guy, the biggest mouse I have ever seen just crawled across the floor.'

I knew instantly that she was telling the truth, but still said, 'You have to be kidding me!'

Vianna said, 'No, I'm not kidding you! It just crawled under the couch.'

I told her to call the management, grumpy because I knew that we were going to have to move rooms at the very least, or at worst find another hotel. From the description she gave me, I knew the creature had been a rat, not a mouse. Without further ado, I began to pack our belongings for the anticipated move.

Vianna rang the management and the man on the other end of the phone calmly told her, 'I am sorry, madam, but every once in a while a rat crawls in from the street and there isn't much we can do about it. I have another room for you if you want it. Would you like to move next door?'

'Do you really think that moving next door will help?' Vianna asked. 'Won't he follow me?'

The man said, 'I can give you a room downstairs if you want.'

Vianna told him that this would be fine, and we moved in the middle of the night, hoping that the whole place wasn't infested with vermin.

We settled in and had no more problems with our stay at the hotel. However, aside from being a rather disagreeable happenstance, the rat was a message to us. We knew from past experiences that all creatures great and small are messages from the universe. The rat told us there were rats stirring in London, of the human variety. We became more alert, and aware that we might be facing challenges in the upcoming soul-mate class.

We'd had replacement class materials and clean clothes sent over from America, but now we learned that British customs were holding them in some nebulous limbo until they got the proper 'itemized list' from us. Presumably they thought we were attempting to bring in clothing for sale or some such activity. After four days of constantly calling the Customs office, I'd finally signed enough forms and made enough of a nuisance of myself for them to give us our packages.

At the Mind, Body, Spirit festival, our ThetaHealing teachers had coordinated a ThetaHealing stand, and we had the opportunity to see some of our friends in Theta. The festival was a grand affair to us, with healing modalities galore. Vianna spoke to a full room of interested people and as usual they loved her. After the class, she signed books at the Hay House stand for a long line of enthusiastic people.

It turned out that there were some challenges with the soul-mate class, but because of our little warning from the rat we were prepared for them, and for the most part the class, while a lot of work, ran relatively smoothly. This was due to some of the teachers who came to help us with coordination. I also had a good crew of nice ladies to help me with the license agreements and certificates.

When the class was over, we relaxed at our hotel, since we had a flight the next day for our debut in Germany.

Germany

We landed in Hamburg, and our pleasant coordinator picked us up at the airport and took us to our first hotel, which had probably been built in the 1920s.

The first night was a little harrowing for Vianna because she soon found out that Hamburg was full of ghosts. The first one she experienced was that of a little girl who was sitting in the street with her head between her legs as she wept. Then she started to see hundreds of tortured souls everywhere – on the streets, in the hallways, on boats in the harbor, all of them sad and lost. That night in the hotel room the ghost of a heavy-set black woman knelt down by Vianna's side of the bed and asked her, 'Will there be anything else that you need tonight, madam?'

Vianna woke me up and told me what had happened to her. She felt she had to move from the old hotel, and after a little hotel shuffling we settled in at one of the most organized establishments we had ever experienced.

This place had fewer ghosts, but Vianna asked me to look up the history of Hamburg to see what had happened to create so many ghosts. When I looked online, I found the city had been bombed at the end of the World War II by the Royal Air Force and in just two days 40,000 people had perished in a firestorm that had been created by the bombs and atmospheric conditions.

When I told Vianna what had happened, she said, 'Of course! That created a vortex in time that trapped the souls of the people who had been killed in the bombing raid.'

After a few days, Vianna got used to seeing so many ghosts and the rest of the trip was uneventful. The hotel had three restaurants in it, and each one was a pleasant dining experience.

ThetaHealing had just been translated into German, and the students said it was a very good translation. We found the Germans to be pleasant, straightforward, psychic, and very much to the point. The class warmed up to Vianna and the students had a very good time. We had two translators, one for the basic class and one for the advanced. Both did a very good job, and I think that overall the German students loved it. We found Hamburg to be a neat and clean city, and there was the added bonus of most people speaking English.

Back to England

We left Germany for England for the last leg of our rather long trip to Europe. After four events, we were tired and hanging on to each other, because when you are on the road that's all you have – each other. When you are together as much as Vianna and I are, you have to learn to get along. Most couples are together for relatively short spans of time. They see one another in the evenings and on the weekends, and sometimes not even then.

Vianna and I joke that we have been together for a lifetime in our 14 years, since we have spent more time together than most other couples have: 24/7 for most of our married life.

When we got to the hotel in London and were settled in, Vianna looked over at me and, in a strange tone of voice, said, 'We have people after us.'

'Are we in danger?' I asked.

'Only through words.'

'Will those words hurt?'

'Not really, but they are aggressive.'

A few minutes later the phone rang and it was our Hay House representative. She told us that people from a news program named *Newsnight* were attempting to get an interview with Vianna. Hay House had refused to set up an interview, knowing the line the program was likely to take, and Vianna was very pleased that her publisher was wise enough to protect her.

She did the Hay House presentation, but we smelled a rat in the crowd. We had the strange feeling that we were being recorded and that someone in the class had a negative agenda.

When the class was over, a lot of people wanted their books signed. I noticed that several of them were asking pointed questions about cancer, so it is likely that they were sent in to gather information. When the book signing was over, we left the building with two of the Hay House team, and because our hotel was around the corner, we opted to walk to it. We were on the last leg of a very long journey, and I knew Vianna was very tired, but it wasn't over yet. The rat's message was indeed revealing itself.

As we left the building, two men came running up from behind us, one with a camera, the other with a microphone.

One was shouting at the top of his lungs, 'Vianna Stibal! Vianna Stibal! Is it true that you claim that you can cure cancer!?' They ran in front of Vianna and attempted to stop her for an interview, pushing a microphone and camera in her face.

At the time I was carrying two bags, Vianna's and mine, so I was a little encumbered otherwise they wouldn't have made it in front of her.

Vianna started to respond to the aggressive interviewer, but I instinctually stepped between them. Vianna grabbed my arm and said, 'Please, please don't hurt them.'

I looked at her and said, 'Vianna, please listen to me. Walk away.'

She repeated, 'Please don't hurt them.'

I said, 'I won't if you walk away.'

Then I firmly but gently moved the interviewer out of her way, telling the two ladies who were walking with us, 'Get her out of here.'

I stayed in front of the two interviewers to give Vianna time to walk away, which she did. She didn't run, but walked briskly away, hand in hand with the other ladies, who by this time were rather upset.

By now, people in the street were yelling at the journalists to leave us alone because of their obvious aggression.

I began to walk away, but at that point the cameraman deemed it necessary to stick his camera in my face. I firmly took hold of the top of it and forced it down, telling him calmly, 'You can't do this.'

The cameraman screamed back at me, 'Yes, we can! This is England, not America!'

I firmly pushed the cameraman behind me and continued down the street. He ran around me to get a parting shot of Vianna as she was walking away.

When we had put the aggressive journalists behind us, we stopped at a donut shop. Vianna commented that it was nice that the people on the street had jumped to our defense without knowing who we were.

The next morning we left for the airport.

That was the end of our trip, but not the end of the story. It seems that there was an agenda behind the whole thing. Several weeks later a story came out 'examining' faith healing, but the program was based on the misconception that it was a question of alternative versus conventional medicine. Vianna works with conventional medicine, not against it.

Someone wrote to our office asking why, out of all the faith-healing modalities, was ThetaHealing getting all the attention?

A fine question.

Afterword

REFLECTIONS

Vianna

Looking back on all the adventures I have had in my life, what I have learned is to be very clear and to distinguish pure knowledge from brain candy. I have learned that there is one energy that moves in all things, an energy that we are intertwined with and connected to. We are part of it and at one with it. I have learned that past-life memories can be explained by this interconnectedness with all things: we can be so in tune with the universe that we are able to access any memories of the past, present, and future. There is the chance that we have lived a life in the past, but that really doesn't matter; we can be connected with that one energy and through it we can have knowledge of all things.

Through God I have had the structure of the Seven Planes of Existence explained to me, so that my mind could grasp the infinite possibilities of All That Is.

I believe that humankind is motivated by love, but sometimes that love is not a good love. Love of money, love of power, love of conflict – the list could go on and on. Real love is love for another person, but there is a risk in this kind of love that most people are unable to take. Nevertheless, this love is the right kind of love and the way to find it is to connect with the All That Is energy.

I have learned that I have a true love, a person who loves me and appreciates me for my eccentricities. It has taken me years to realize that he isn't going to fade away or disappear. It is extraordinary to realize that someone might love you completely as a compatible soul mate, that you might feel intensely connected to someone, to a depth that is divine in nature, re-creating a relationship that is felt unto the soul, so that both of you feel as though you could be parts of one being, a stronger being. The love for a soul mate is an eternal one that is so powerful that it transcends death itself and is reborn with new life, refusing the separation imposed by the indifference of death.

There was a time after the coma when I would only eat the food that Guy prepared for me. Any other food I wouldn't touch because I couldn't feel the energy of love and concern in it, so I knew that it wouldn't nourish me.

Guy and I have had the worst of times and the best of times, and we still have each other.

Guy

Hand in hand, Vianna and I have traveled and witnessed many things:

The Red Sand Beach and the Rattling Beach of Maui, Hawaii
The secret burial-place of the goddess Pele, Maui, Hawaii
The mother tree of Maui, Hawaii
The Shroud of Turin, Italy
Saint Peter's Basilica and the Sistine Chapel, Italy
The remains of the Buddha, Japan
The chambers under the Pyramid of the Sun, Mexico
The temple-birthplace of the god Krishna, India
A wild leopard, India
Castles and palaces, Britain and Ireland
The mists of Avalon, England
Stonehenge and Avebury, England
Rosslyn Chapel, Scotland
The Isle of Skye, Scotland
Newgrange, Ireland
The Hill of Tara, Ireland
Bridget's Well, Ireland
The Cliffs of Moher, Ireland
The ancient books of the sagas, Iceland
Ayers rock (Uluru), Australia
Camels at sunset, Australia
The Great Barrier Reef, Australia
The birthplace of Nikola Tesla, Croatia
The Long White Cloud of New Zealand
The hot pools of Rotorua, New Zealand
The Grand Canyon, Arizona
Mesa Verde, Colorado
A Buddhist temple, New York
The Empire State Building, New York

The beaches of Florida
Redwood and the sequoia trees in California
Mount Shasta, California
The Olympic Range, Washington
The sweat lodge of a Paiute medicine man, Utah
Bryce Canyon and the dripping spring at Zion National
  Park, Utah

We have walked through these places and many more on our journey together.

As I reflect upon my union with Vianna, I have come to realize it is transience itself that is our challenge. The very essence that is life brings us to the challenge of the body, with its limitations. These limitations are what drives us, as much as the need for food. When a certain point is reached, no material food will fill the needs of the spirit. Even in the physical act of eating, food gives us less and less pleasure until we realize that the food we are after is that first taste of spiritual white lightning, the *soma* from the sacred tree.

Some people, I have come to realize, are a sort of white lightning. They are at once clear and pure, angry and sad, darkness and light, all in one breath. Once you drink of them, they are unforgettable. You are intoxicated with the taste of their heady essence and other people are like lesser derivatives. There is no escaping that they are the pure quill, the original *soma* from the sacred tree that we all drink from, and in their fearless intensity they burn through your veins, to be quenched by the mortal bounds of the body, but the residue remains. These people remind us that while the needs of our body are unquenchable and boundless beyond filling, this one bolt of spiritual lightning fills us with spiritual energy enough to give meaning to our illusionary anguish of mortality. I believe that is what happened when I first kissed Vianna. That first kiss was to me a taste of the Philosopher's Stone, that alchemical union of polarities, male and female essences coming together to create one whole, and for that brief moment, I felt it. To me, this is what true soul mates are all about.

Many people talk about Cupid and his arrows, which instill in the victim an overwhelming love for another person. But Vianna and I both believe that it is fairy dust from the love pixies that is sprinkled on us periodically to remind us that in spite of all the limitations of mortality, we still love one another. Both of us believe that we were meant to be together and whenever things become stressful between us, the order goes out once again to sprinkle us with a new libation of love dust, suffusing our senses and giving us a reminder that in spite of all the vicissitudes that life has to offer, our love is eternal.

As for where we are now, it is living a life that goes on...

Both of my boys are now grown men. As of 2011, Andy is 30 years old and Tyrel, 21. Both have finally reached a point where they have come to terms with themselves and their world.

After many years in prison, Andy returned home in 2010 a changed man with a fierce sense of loyalty to his family and the desire to get his life together. He loves animals and children and is always ready to right any wrong done to others. He can see the potential in others and has a lot of psychic abilities. When he got together with a woman named Dawn, we saw that he had changed. She decided to let him work for us at Nature's Path. Dawn's three children have sweet dispositions that make them easy to love and they bring Vianna the joy she so deserves. With Andy's daughter, they have four kids altogether.

Tyrel is doing well and is also putting his life together after years of being in and out of jail. He is as strong as an ox and fast as an eel. He is fascinated by antiques of all kinds and seems to like old people.

There is a fury inside both of these boys, a furnace that burns hot and that as a father I cannot quench. Time will have to douse some of the fire inside them. With time, they will find goodness. In both of them, however, their wildness has changed to a sense of protectiveness of Vianna and her work.

In 2010 my father gifted the farm in Roberts, Idaho, to Vianna and me. The place needed a lot of work – the old house needed renovating, and I knew that making it a farm once again would take time, especially considering the thousands of cattle that had wintered on the land. But I had come full circle.

And so it was that in the summer of 2011 I suddenly came back into myself as I leaned on my shovel in the middle of a field of wheat as the irrigation water flowed around my rubber boots and I was a farmer once more. As I stood there, I contemplated all that had happened to me since I fell in love with Vianna on that fateful day. As I reflected on the almost overwhelming events of the years since I began my adventure, I wondered once again if it was real or something conjured from my overactive imagination. All the events, faces, and places seemed surreal, as though they had happened to someone else whose life I had experienced vicariously, watching as one would a reality television show. Inevitably, all that had happened had led me back to the person that I have always been and always will be at heart, the mountain boy fascinated by the mystical, the guy Vianna calls her man from Montana.

On April 6, 2011, we were blessed with a new baby, Elixander Shyne, born to Brandy and Chris. His calm energy has brought a sense of harmony to the institute and to all who work there. If someone at the institute has a baby, Vianna lets them set up daycare in the office so that the 'baby magic' will permeate the place. Brandy has an incredible family comprised of her three little boys, Remington, Kai, and now Shyne.

The summer of 2011 was an abundant one, with the classes at the institute some of the best ever. In the fall we went back to Mexico and then to Australia. Both classes went smoothly and we looked forward to 2012, since we had never believed in the end-of-the-world scenario put forward by some. To us, 2012 is a new beginning, the cornucopia of abundance that we have been waiting for.

We spent seven weeks in India in the beginning of 2012, teaching a whirlwind of classes. There is something about the spiritual energy of India that seems to feed Vianna, but really it is the love that matters.

In the first part of 2012 Joshua finally won joint custody of his children. We are full of hope that Lindsey can move on with her life now in a healthy way, without hatred and anger, at least for the sake of the children.

One of the very best things that has happened in 2012 has been that on March 10 Bobbi gave birth to a baby boy, Andrew Xavier Lott. We call him AXL. This brings Bobbi's family to four: Bobbi herself, Brennan, Jena, and AXL. New life is the essence of abundance, and little babies show us that life goes forward.

In all these years, I have never seen Vianna so happy and full of life! We are both learning to make time stand still, or at least slow it down a little, so that we can enjoy the faces and the places just a little longer!

Appendix I

VIANNA'S PLAYLIST

Music has always been significant to Vianna. The music that has played in her life has been a symbol of the memorable times she has experienced. She has compiled a playlist of songs that relate to the noteworthy events in this story:

- Teenage years: Elton John, 'Tiny Dancer'
- First marriage: Bread, 'Baby I'm-a Want You'
- Nuclear Security Training: Yanni, 'Within Attraction'
- Second marriage: Roy Orbison, 'You Got It'
- First office: Olivia Newton-John, 'Magic'
- Divorced the third time: Shawn Mullins, 'Lullaby'
- Guy: Savage Garden, 'I Knew I Loved You,' Edwin McCain, 'I Could Not Ask for More'
- The coma: Tonic, 'If You Could Only See,' Rush, 'Time Stand Still'
- Bobbi's wedding: George Strait, 'I Cross My Heart'

- The enemies attack: Otis Taylor 'Ten Million Slaves' (*Public Enemies* soundtrack)
- Conquering fears: Richard Blackmore/Candice Night, 'Locked within the Crystal Ball'

Appendix 2

MEDICAL CORRESPONDENCE

When I was diagnosed with cancer by the University of Utah in 1995, I was automatically registered in the Huntsman Cancer Hospital Registry. The following letter will be sent to me annually for the rest of my life until the Huntsman Institute receives notification of my death, either via a death certificate or by Medicare.

Today my femur continues to be healthy and I am free of cancer.

University Health Care
Hospitals & Clinics

August 16, 2010

Vianna Stibal
354 N 4400 E
RIGBY, ID 83442

Dear Vianna Stibal:

As a former patient of the Huntsman Cancer Institute and University of Utah Health Care, we have a continuing interest in your health. This letter is our chance to find out how you're doing, as well as remind you about the importance of an annual physical examination.

Please take a few moments to answer the questions below. The information will be used by our researchers and clinicians to improve the care of our patients. Your information will be kept confidential.

What is the condition of your general health at the present time? _____

_____

Have you had any further medical or surgical treatment relating to your tumor since leaving this hospital? If so, please briefly describe: _____

_____

Who is your current physician? _____

If your address listed above is not correct, please provide:

Current Address: _____

_____

Phone Number: _____

Please provide the name, address and phone number of a person(s) not living with you who will know your current address and telephone number. _____

_____

Relationship: _____

If you are unable to complete this questionnaire, it would be greatly appreciated if you could obtain the assistance of a friend or relative and supply as much information as possible.

Any further comments you may wish to make may be written on the reverse side of this letter. A return envelope is enclosed for your convenience. Thank you for taking the time to respond to our patient information letter. We at the Huntsman Cancer Institute and University of Utah Health Care are genuinely interested in your health and look forward to hearing from you soon.

Sincerely yours,

Follow-up Services
Huntsman Cancer Hospital Cancer Registry
1950 E Circle of Hope, SLC, UT 84112

Figure 1: Huntsman Cancer Institute and University of Utah Health Care patient follow-up letter.

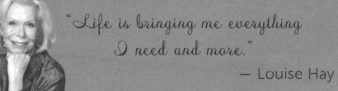

ABOUT THE AUTHORS

Vianna Stibal is the renowned author of the books *ThetaHealing*, *Advanced ThetaHealing*, and *ThetaHealing Diseases and Disorders*. She is recognized worldwide as an inspirational speaker on the art of self-healing through focused prayer. In this book she teams up with her husband, Guy, to tell their true-life soul-mate story.

Guy Stibal is a former rancher, historian, writer, romantic, and follower of the bright knowledge in all things. He has been the spiritual inspiration for Vianna since 1998 when they found one another and went on the wings of prayer to create ThetaHealing.

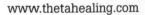